The Pride and the Fall
Iran 1974–1979

The Pride and the Fall
Iran 1974–1979

Anthony Parsons

JONATHAN CAPE
THIRTY BEDFORD SQUARE LONDON

First published 1984
Reprinted 1984 (three times)
Copyright © 1984 Anthony Parsons

Jonathan Cape, 30 Bedford Square, London WC1

British Library Cataloguing in Publication Data
Parsons, *Sir* Anthony
The pride and the fall.
1. Iran—Politics and government—1941–1979
I. Title
955′053′0924   DS318

ISBN 0-224-02196-6

The author and publishers are grateful to the following for permission to reproduce extracts in the text: Faber and Faber Ltd and Harcourt Brace Jovanovich, Inc. for excerpts from 'East Coker', p. 1, 'The Dry Salvages', p. 131, and 'Burnt Norton', p. 151, all of which were taken from *Four Quartets* by T. S. Eliot, copyright © 1943 by T. S. Eliot, renewed 1971 by Esme Valerie Eliot.

Printed and bound in Great Britain
by Butler & Tanner Ltd, Frome and London

I dedicate this book to my family, my strongest supporters and sternest critics; especially my wife and younger son for their comments on the first draft, most of which I have incorporated, and my daughter-in-law for undertaking the burdensome task of typing my original manuscript.

Contents

Preface

Princess Paley, unlike my other critics, has rendered me one
service for which I am grateful. I have often wondered what
was the motive that prompted me to start the Russian Revolution, and she is good enough to tell me.

Sir George Buchanan, *My Mission to Russia*

This book is a personal record. It has no pretensions to
scholarship: indeed the dramatic history of Iran in the 1970s
is still too close for the scholar's lens to be brought into focus
on it. Nor is it a full factual history of Iran in the last years of
the Shah, including the revolution. Many such books have
already appeared, some written by journalists and quasi-
academics, some by those who need, for reasons of self-
esteem, to justify themselves and their perception of events
– after the events have taken place; some by those who feel
compelled for personal or political reasons to place the blame
for the collapse of the Shah's regime on outside, exotic
forces. My motives are different. First, I have to exorcise the
memory of what was without doubt the most absorbing and
compelling experience of my diplomatic life – what better
way to do this than to set it down on paper? Second, and
more important, I want to find the answers to certain questions which have plagued me since I left Tehran towards the
end of January 1979, a few days after the Shah and his family
had flown away into exile. Could I, as British Ambassador,
have been more perceptive in the years before the revolution
broke out? Could I have anticipated that the forces of opposition to the Shah – the religious classes, the bazaar, the students – would combine to destroy him, although each of these

ix

groups was hostile to the regime for a different reason? Could I have known in advance that the combination of these civilian, unarmed, elements would prove too strong for a regime whose power was based on united, well armed, well equipped and loyal armed forces backed by what appeared to be a formidable security apparatus – the dreaded SAVAK? And, if I had been able to see so deep into the heart of Iranian society, would I have advised my government, as well as the British private and public sectors, to adopt different policies – different in all fields including our political and strategic relationship with the Shah, our commercial and financial links with Iran, oil, the sale of military equipment, etc.? And again, if we had adopted different policies across the broad spectrum of our dealings with Iran, would this have lessened the damage to British interests when the collapse came? All these are questions which need to be asked, and I shall do my best to answer them honestly.

I dedicate this book to many people: to my close Iranian friends, notably Amir Abbas Hoveyda, Gholamreza Nikpay and Abbas Ali Khalatbari who went to their deaths with exemplary courage and dignity in the aftermath of the revolution, and to the many others whom I knew personally who faced the firing squads: to my valued Iranian friends now living in exile with whom I have had so many discussions of the events through which we lived together: and lastly to all those Iranians who remain convinced that Britain and America, or perhaps America and Britain, plotted and brought about the downfall of the Shah and the installation of Ayatollah Khomeini as his replacement. 'I mourn for the tragedy of my country,' wrote an Iranian lady to me in 1979, 'but the great powers wished it so, and what could we do?' How many times did the Shah say to me in the closing months 'The people are saying that, if you lift up Khomeini's beard, you will find MADE IN ENGLAND written under his chin.' For all his disclaimers, he clearly was disposed to believe this folklore himself. On the day I left Tehran for good, a middle-aged Iranian, educated in Britain, and long married to an English-woman, went so far as to suggest to a member of my staff that the country would have peace if only the Americans would behave like sportsmen and admit defeat at the hands of Britain. According to this gentleman, we had never forgiven the United States for breaking our oil monopoly in Iran in the early 1950s. We had patiently bided our time – for a quarter of a century – and had at last seen our way clear to strike. Naturally we had made use of the mullahs, the traditional agents of the British, to bring down the Shah, latterly the creature of the United States. We had won: the Shah had gone, and our man, Khomeini, was on his way back. My counsellor asked whether it would be any use his suggesting that this theory was utter nonsense. 'But of course you have to say that. I know. I was educated in your country and am married to an English lady. You cannot deceive me.'

I fear that these numerous Iranians, that is to say those who accept this conventional Iranian wisdom as gospel, will find my narrative disappointing. It contains no revelations of sinister machinations against the Shah and his government, of secret plotting between myself and the ayatollahs of Qom and Mashhad. Nor do I explain why Britain should have adopted a policy so destructive of our national interest. Those flattering believers in the omnipresence of the British hidden hand will find my story naive and unconvincing. I hope that they will at least give me credit for taking so much trouble, even in my retirement, to throw more dust in their eyes.

ONE

The Background to My Mission

> There is, it seems to us,
> At best, only a limited value
> In the knowledge derived from experience.
> The knowledge imposes a pattern and falsifies.
>
> T.S. Eliot, 'East Coker'

The Middle East crisis of the autumn of 1973 was in full swing when I was summoned one day from my desk at the Foreign Office to see the Head of Administration. I was frantically busy and resentful of the need to switch my mind to some administrative question. I walked over to his room in a surly mood, only to be told that, subject to the usual formalities, I would be the next Ambassador to Tehran. Was I surprised? Certainly: I had expected to spend another year in London as the Middle East Under-Secretary and then, if I thought about it at all, perhaps to be appointed Ambassador to an Arab country or to Turkey, scenes of my earlier service. I had never served in Iran and had never imagined that such luck would come my way.

How would I define the perfect overseas posting for a professional diplomat? There are many countries which are agreeable to live in, where the people and government are friendly, but where British interests are negligible; personal life is pleasant but official duties are limited and boring. There are countries where the opposite is true, where there are substantial British interests which respond to active diplomacy, but a hostile or restricted environment, perhaps a

1

vile climate; in such places, family life can pay a heavy price for professional fulfilment. It is rare that all positive qualities combine in one place – an absorbingly interesting and challenging job, a country in the process of dynamic economic and social change but still aglow with the light of a long and colourful past, and endless opportunities to explore places vivid with spectacular scenic contrast and redolent of historical romance, hitherto only names in books – the Caspian Sea, Shiraz, Isfahan, Persepolis. As my wife and I saw it in the autumn of 1973, the Embassy in Tehran offered this perfect combination of qualities and we prepared ourselves for the future in a mood of excitement and delight.

I confess that I was also a trifle apprehensive about certain aspects of my embassy to Tehran. I knew the Shah slightly and respected his intelligence and authority. But I shrank a little from the prospect of the stiffness and grandeur of the Pahlavi Court, the dressing up in uniform and the rigid protocol and formality; all striking contrasts to the informality of the Arab world to which I was accustomed. Fortunately the Prime Minister, Amir Abbas Hoveyda, was a personal friend of mine of fifteen years' standing and I knew and liked several of his ministers and senior officials from my dealings with Iran at the FCO. But might the Iranians not resent my Arab past? I knew that they were touchily proud of their Aryan origins and held their Arab neighbours in some contempt. Might they not think that a British diplomat from the Paris/Washington circuit would be a more suitable envoy than someone with a long string of Arab capitals in his curriculum vitae?

However, these were minor anxieties which did little or nothing to dampen my enthusiasm. Iran had all the fascination for me that it has exerted over Englishmen for centuries, perhaps more so because my knowledge of the country was vicarious. I had also been directly engaged in the formulation of British policy towards Iran for nearly three years and was fully conscious of its importance for my country – as a source of crude oil, as a strategic partner in a turbulent part of the world, as a rapidly growing market for British exports, both civil and military. My experience told me that personal diplomacy could play a part in promoting these interests.

What of the internal situation and the prospects for the Shah's regime in this country in which Britain had so much at stake - the subject of this book? From my vantage point in the Foreign Office, I was well placed, as I prepared to leave for Tehran, to review Whitehall's perception of Iran in the early 1970s. There were several negative factors. The human rights record of the Shah's regime was bad. Arbitrary arrest, detention without trial, torture, summary executions, and the persecution of recalcitrant students and workers were commonplace. But when had they not been so in Iran and, for that matter, in many countries in the region? Was the Shah's government any worse than many others with which Britain had close relations, or did it simply appear to be so because he insisted on Iran being judged by Western standards as part of the Western world? I would no doubt form a clearer view on the spot.

We knew that the religious classes were implacably opposed to the Shah's vision of an Iran transformed into a modern, industrialised Western state. We knew that the Shah's dictatorial and repressive system of government had generated resentment and sullenness in the growing student body. There were small terrorist groups at large which occasionally carried out assassinations, usually of SAVAK personnel or American military officers. There was trouble in many university campuses. But none of these manifestations seemed to command broad popular support and there was no pattern of increase in violent incidents.

On balance the Shah appeared to be more than holding his own in the race to outdistance the forces of opposition through rapid social and economic development designed to transform the material situation of his people. He had out-manoeuvred and neutralised all those elements with which he had originally been in competition and with which he had been obliged to share power. The old political parties had been replaced by a charade of democracy of his own creation. The tribal chiefs and landowning grandees had been reduced to impotence by the land reforms of the 1960s, and the opposition of the religious classes had been scotched: they had not offered a serious challenge to the regime since the bloody quelling of the Tehran bazaar riots in 1963. The government consisted of technocrats without political constituencies, wholly dependent on the Shah's will. The armed forces and security services were united and loyal to their Commander-in-Chief, the Shah. On the whole, Iran over the previous decade had been a model of tranquillity compared to most other countries in the Third World and, with the enhanced prospects for development arising from the oil price increase, there appeared to be no reason why the Shah should not continue to forge ahead.

Our principal anxiety was that the regime had become over-dependent on the Shah as a person and that his sudden removal from the scene, through assassination, illness or accident, would create a dangerous power vacuum. By the same token, we felt that he had become excessively isolated and dependent on the support of his armed and security forces. It was difficult to see how he could expect to realise his vision of a fundamental social and economic transformation of Iranian society without a concomitant political transformation, that is to say without enabling his people to participate in the decision-making processes which were so powerfully affecting their lives.

I resolved to examine all these premises closely when I had settled down in Tehran. Quite apart from the professional necessity to offer sound advice to Whitehall and to the British private and public sectors on the domestic situation, I had a keen intellectual interest in observing at first hand the prospects of one of the few Third World countries which was generally believed to be close to breaking through the barrier of underdevelopment. Many people spoke to me during my briefing period of Iran as the next Japan, or South Korea, or Brazil. Could this be true? The country undoubtedly had firm leadership; what I had seen of the Iranian governmental and entrepreneurial establishment had impressed me; there was now no shortage of money. Political continuity was probably the key to the success or failure of the Shah's ambitions.

I realised that our observation of the internal scene must be conducted with discretion. My principal objective was to continue the work of building a close and normal relationship with the Shah and his government, untrammelled by overtones of the past. The British had a not undeserved reputation

4

for interfering in Iran's domestic affairs for over a century. We were alleged to have helped to bring the Shah's father to the throne and we had of course been directly involved in his abdication in 1941 and his son's succession. We were traditionally associated with the Iranian religious classes and with other political groupings now opposed to the Shah. All this lay in the past behind the watershed of the nationalisation of Iranian oil under Mossadegh in the early 1950s and the subsequent reconciliation after his fall from power; but Iranian memories were long and the Shah's complexes about Britain were still close to the surface of his mind. I needed therefore to observe the political scene without arousing any suspicion of improper involvement in Iran's internal affairs or of making clandestine contacts which, if discovered, would severely damage our relationship with the Shah. There would be no 'spying on Iran' in my Embassy.

TWO

1974–1975

They hated and despised the imperial power, but most of them were ready to cringe before it. Yes, even the best were over-awed by the real might under the tinsel of that greatness.

Joseph Conrad, *Suspense*

It did not take me long to discover that, whatever benefits the Shah's policies might be bringing to the people of Iran, happiness was not one of them, at least in Tehran. Wonderfully situated at the foot of the towering, snow-capped Elburz range of mountains, Tehran in 1974 was a monument to all that is worst in the achievements of modern man. Ugly, sprawling, shoddy, undistinguished, pullulating with cars and people, buried under a cloud of pollution, it must have been one of the most repulsive capital cities in the world. The city pulsated with activity of all kinds, construction, demolition, commerce, industry, government, all the indicators of a booming economy; but the people as a whole seemed surly, lacklustre and neurotic. The slow, traditional courtesies of the Muslim world were being swamped by the onrush of the Great Civilisation, but were not being replaced by the vitality and enthusiasm which might have been expected in a society in the process of rapid and fundamental change.

What was this Great Civilisation which was daily trumpeted in the strictly controlled press, radio and television? The Shah had invented the phrase, which probably sounds more preposterous in English than in Persian, in 1972 and had subsequently declared that it would be achieved by the end of the 1980s. It was essentially materialistic, the realisation of the Shah's vision of Iran as a fully developed, indus-

6

trial state, the Japan of Central Asia. But it was more than that. In the Shah's mind, Iran was part of Western civilisation, separated by an accident of geography from its natural partners and equals. The Iranians in his view were Aryan, not Semitic, and their innate talents and abilities had been suffocated by the blanket of the Arab invasion 1,200 years previously and its spiritual concomitant, Islam. He saw it as his mission to lift this blanket and to restore Iran to its former grandeur among the Great Powers. Hence the Great Civilisation was not simply a question of raising the material standard of living of the Iranian people, although this was its most obvious manifestation. It had a strong psychological connotation. The Iranians were to be galvanised out of their slow, traditional Muslim way of life and projected into the Western Europe of the twenty-first century, all under his personal, inspired leadership. The closest parallel in the modern history of the region was Mustafa Kemal Atatürk's regeneration of Turkey out of the ashes of the Ottoman Empire following the First World War. Atatürk had deliberately reached back into the Turkish, as opposed to Islamic, origins of the inhabitants of the Anatolian plateau. He had Europeanised the country by altering its traditional dress, by reforming the Turkish language and replacing the Arabic with the Latin script, by starting a programme of industrialisation, by establishing European political institutions, and so on. One of his greatest admirers had been the Shah's father, Reza Shah, whose son saw himself as having been chosen to fulfil his father's dream.

By the second half of 1974 I felt able to draw some tentative conclusions about the impact of these revolutionary policies (let there be no doubt, the Shah *was* a revolutionary) on the Iranian people, and about the possibility of the Shah being able to translate his ambitious vision into reality. There was no doubt that a great deal had been and was being achieved, particularly with the removal of previous financial constraints. The whole country was engulfed in a frenzy of activity. Most cities and towns now had rapidly growing industrial estates and, particularly in the provinces, the old urban centres, based on the traditional bazaars, were being complemented by modern quarters and housing estates serving the new commercial and manufacturing sectors. But the boom which began in early 1974 was already producing strains and contradictions. The massive injection of new money into the economy following the oil price rise of December 1973, without any corresponding increase in production, had led to serious inflation – even the government admitted to an annual inflation rate of 20 per cent and the true figure was much higher. Iran's primitive railway system was overwhelmed, the few small ports were choked, the medieval organisation for internal distribution of goods was totally inadequate and shortages of the commonest consumer products were not infrequent. It was clear that these symptoms of over-rapid expansion were jeopardising the Shah's plans by threatening the stability of the social structure of the country. Peasants were pouring into the cities seeking the streets that were allegedly paved with gold, but not finding them, and instead becoming a rootless, badly housed urban proletariat. Skilled manpower was in desperately short supply, as the embryonic mass education system lagged further behind the rocketing demand. The new middle class, the principal beneficiaries of Pahlavi rule outside the very rich, were suffering the effects of inflation: it was, for example, normal for a middle manager or equivalent government official to be paying up to 70 per cent of his total salary on rent alone. The exotic radicalism and grandiose scale of some of the Shah's pet projects were disrupting the lives and livelihoods of elements of the rural population and thus causing resentment and dissidence.

Iran in 1974 was a land of bewildering contrasts. I would visit a modern factory and come away feeling that I had seen something on a par with its equivalent in Western Europe – could it be that the Great Civilisation was possible? I would visit a teeming bazaar which left me with the impression that nothing had changed in this most traditional of countries. I saw the docks at Khorramshahr at the head of the Persian Gulf and left despairing that order could ever be produced out of the amorphous mountains of machinery, bags of sugar, piles of solidified cement, and assorted consumer goods, a sight which would have daunted the god Hercules. I saw Persian villages rooted in the immemorial tradition of peasant life, contrasting with an area of massive, mainly foreign-owned agri-businesses where the old villages had been bulldozed to facilitate the use of agricultural machinery, leaving surly peasants grouped in centralised, landless collections of modern huts – there had been serious outbreaks of sabotage of the new machines in that place. I had visited a game reserve, established on the Western pattern for the propagation of wildlife, from which the pastoral tribes who had grazed the land for centuries had been driven, to be arrested and imprisoned if they dared to return with their flocks; but in spite of being an area where the killing of game was forbidden, it was in fact used by members of the regime as a hunting ground. I had seen the vulgar ostentation of the *nouveau riche* in North Tehran and the sickening squalor of the masses in South Tehran. I had also seen how the centre of the city was genuinely developing into a middle-class area – the cars which choked the streets were the locally assembled (British) cars of the middle class, not the Cadillacs of the rich. I had seen the Shah's power base in the new military housing estates and modern barracks in Tehran and the provinces, in the arrogance of Iranian officers and soldiers in the streets and shops of Tehran. I had watched the brilliant spectacle of the Asian Games in the magnificent stadium built to accommodate the Olympic Games in 1984, and I had been aware that about 10,000 students had been arbitrarily arrested by SAVAK for the period of the Asian Games 'in case they made trouble'. Memories of the Munich Olympics were still fresh. I had visited schools and universities where I was made conscious of the scale of the education explosion which the Shah had launched, and of the discontent and hostility to the regime on many campuses where SAVAK Land-Rovers appeared to be a permanent feature. I had been staggered by the hectic activity generated by the oil boom, and shocked by the scale of the corruption which it had engendered. I had noted fists being shaken as I passed the Holy Shrine at Qom and had sensed the fanatical devotion of the pilgrims to the great shrine at Mashhad, as well as the open contempt of the newly appointed provincial governor for the whole Islamic tradition. The sombre, introverted faces of the mullahs in the Tehran streets contrasted vividly with the cosmopolitanism

9

of life in the houses of the technocrats and entrepreneurs in the northern suburbs.

Yes, a great deal was happening and Iranian society was undoubtedly in the throes of change. The overall standard of living was beginning to rise: a new middle class and a new, and well paid, class of industrial workers were emerging. The armed forces were united, strong, well-equipped and loyal; the apparatus of the police state was ubiquitous and ruthless. The Shah was resolute, autocratic and in full control. It was hard to imagine how his regime could be overthrown; even if he fell to accident, sudden illness or the assassin's bullet, the likelihood was that, after a short period of stagnation and political uncertainty while the forces of intrigue, in-fighting and opposition resolved themselves, strong central government would reassert itself under the regency of the Empress, backed by the armed forces, pending the coming of age of his son. Iran, in my judgment at the end of 1974, was as good a bet for Britain as most countries of the world. There were of course risks, but they should not deter us from taking advantage of the formidable commercial opportunities which the Shah's accelerated pursuit of the Great Civilisation had opened up.

Of course I had many reservations, but they were directed to the longer term. It was obvious that there was no hope of the Shah achieving his goals in his short time scale. 'The drive to the Great Civilisation is like dropping ink onto a large cloth. The stains spread but they will never colour the whole cloth,' as one of my staff put it to me. The strains and disruptions caused by the boom were manifest – 'The oil price increase was a catastrophe for Iran,' a wise Iranian banker told me in mid-1974 – and many of the Shah's favourite projects were absurdly unrealistic and irrelevant to his country's needs. He was not popular, except perhaps amongst the new rich, the rising middle class and the industrial workers; the students and religious classes were hostile. There was some minor terrorist violence and inflation was vitiating the rising expectations of all classes of society. Government was oppressive and corrupt, in many areas incompetent. Perhaps most significant was the Shah's failure to energise his people behind his policies. Sycophancy and acquiescence were the most positive manifestations while sullen passivity was the most preponderant. He wanted his people to use more initiative at all levels but was not prepared to delegate authority. He was in too much of a hurry to risk the delays which genuine public debate and discussion would impose on the fulfilment of his dream. Many Iranians took this autocratic style for granted but it was increasingly resented by those in the liberal tradition, particularly the young and Western educated who should have been his most dynamic constituency. Hence, as time pressed more heavily on his heels, the Shah had become less inclined to trust even his ministerial technocrats. Parliament had become even more of a servile rubber stamp, the press more closely controlled, governmental propaganda more bombastic and arrogant, the secret police more pervasive.

So closed 1974, the most sensational year in the recent history of Iran, certainly in the twenty-year period since the Shah re-established his leadership after the fall of Dr Mossadegh in 1953. My broad advice to the British business and financial community ran on the following lines:

> This is a Third World country and there is no Third World country where a sudden change of regime should be a matter for surprise. If you do business here you must accept that risk. Therefore sell where you can and do not invest unless you cannot sell without doing so. If you have to invest, keep it to the minimum and choose industries where your profits derive from exports from Britain - assembly plants - rather than from Iran. Within these limits I believe that Iran is as good a market as you will find in the Third World, and a great deal better than most.

We were all surprised at the short duration of the boom. By mid-1975 it was over and Iran was heading for a budgetary deficit of nearly $2 billion. As the recession in the West deepened, the demand for oil fell. Rocketing inflation at home and abroad, combined with dollar depreciation, had severely reduced Iran's purchasing power. Projects which had been estimated in hundreds of millions of dollars were now costing

11

billions. Corruption, the flight of capital abroad, shortages of manpower at all levels and infrastructural bottlenecks compounded the problems. The voracious demands of the armed forces and of the doubled fifth Five Year Plan entered into competition. By the summer some of the more grandiose and unattainable projects had been dropped or severely pruned. Enterprises such as the creation of thousands of hospital beds in hospitals to be built, equipped and staffed entirely by foreigners were cancelled. The reorganisation of Iran's distribution system was abandoned. The Shah's disastrous foray into the international sugar market died in a welter of recrimination. The thousands of American transport vehicles which the Shah had ordered to clear the congestion at the Persian Gulf ports sank deeper into the salt flats of Bandarabbas. There had never been drivers for them and now there never would be. Price became for the first time a major feature in the letting of contracts. Government expenditure was cut and virtually all civilian projects had their completion dates extended. Domestic price controls were instituted; gangs of vigilantes were recruited to intimidate merchants into reducing their prices. An anti-corruption drive was launched and some minor entrepreneurs and bazaar merchants were punished – even one of the Shah's relations had to lie low for a time. Foreign firms were required to sign affidavits declaring how much money and to whom they had paid 'commissions' on their contracts. In short, it was a year of sobering reappraisal after the frenzied expectations of 1974. Only the armed forces were immune from the cold wind of austerity, Persian style.

The disappointment of the exaggerated expectations of 1974 was accompanied by a palpable political malaise which permeated all important sectors of Iranian society. In August, I felt the need to modify the relatively rosy picture which I had painted to London in the boom year of 1974. The terrorist groups, politically implacable and combining radical elements of the extreme right and the extreme left, were operating with increased efficiency, sophistication and coordination. In the first half of 1975 there were as many as twelve political assassinations, including two American military officers and a member of the staff of the American

Embassy. There was an upsurge of bombings in the provinces, including explosions at the Iran-American Society and the British Council in Mashhad. SAVAK was capable of containing this violence, but not of eliminating it. More serious, there had been strikes and violent demonstrations at a number of universities including those in the urban centres of Tehran, Shiraz, Tabriz and Ahwaz. The educated youth was seriously alienated and a link was discernible between the intelligentsia as a whole and the extreme terrorist groups. The universities were overcrowded, poorly staffed and badly taught. Resentment at corruption, nepotism, the suppression of freedom and overt political activity left the students with no outlet except in militancy. Thus, the principal contacts between the mass of the students and the authorities were the baton charges, beatings up and wholesale arrests of SAVAK and the police. This phenomenon naturally accelerated the process of alienation.

The religious classes too, who had never forgiven the Shah and his father for trying to break their power and who deeply resented and feared the transformation of Iranian society away from Islam and towards a Western, secular model, were at best neutral and passive, at worst obstructive and dissident. They knew that their influence amongst the still deeply religious masses was strong, but feared the Shah's heavy hand and his readiness to use it. But there were amongst them men of character who could if they dared lend considerable support to the extremist groups whose philosophy contained elements of Islamic fundamentalism.

It was difficult to assess where the bazaaris, the guardians of the traditional economy of Iran and still the preponderant urban majority, stood. The bazaar had for centuries provided the raw material for the urban mobs which had periodically menaced and broken successive regimes. The bazaaris were suffering from the high rate of inflation and were apprehensive that their livelihoods would be destroyed by the modern sector of the economy which the Shah was deliberately promoting. The bazaar was a potent weapon for any agitator and comprised the sector from which the religious classes could most easily whip up support. The Shah had in the past dealt ruthlessly with bazaar riots, most recently in 1963 when they

13

were suppressed at a cost of hundreds of lives. For the moment, the bazaaris were quiet and my view was that the Shah would deal firmly with any future trouble from that quarter.

There were some positive features from the point of view of the regime. In my judgment the peasant villagers and tribesmen, who probably comprised over 50 per cent of the population of Iran, were on balance better off under the Pahlavis. Life had changed little in the average Iranian village, but what change there had been was for the better. There were now village schools throughout the country, small clinics, some piped water and electricity. Feeder roads had been built, connecting remote villages with local towns. The transistor radio and the motor cycle were common features of village life and the peasants were no longer serfs to absentee landlords and their exacting local agents. Above all, for the first time in centuries, strong central government had pacified the country: it was now possible to travel throughout Iran unescorted and unmolested. The peasantry were too used to the arbitrariness and cruelty of government to resent actively their continuation under the present regime. On the other hand the villages were too small and too scattered, over 60,000 in a country the size of Western Europe, to organise or to be organised either in support of or against the regime. They were not a significant factor, except in so far as they were being drained to swell the growing urban mass of the population.

More important was the increasing, but still relatively small, class of organised labour in the new, manufacturing industries which the Shah's programmes were creating in the vicinity of all cities and towns. They were, in spite of inflation and the confused muddle of the boom, far better off than their fathers would have dreamed possible. The shortage of labour had given them economic power, and cash wages and fringe benefits were rising rapidly, in some cases to Western European levels. They had no need of independent trade unions to improve their lot. Employers had to compete vigorously to retain their labour forces who, if their demands were refused, simply moved to the factory next door. High wages, workers' low cost housing, creches for the children, and paid holidays were becoming common features and the industrial working class and their families seemed to be busily occupied in establishing themselves in the modern, consumer society. They had no material reason for following any call to rise and overthrow the regime which had done so much to establish them in their new-found affluence.

The main beneficiaries of the march towards the Great Civilisation were undoubtedly the armed forces and the new monied upper and middle classes – the technocrats, government officials, industrialists, bankers, entrepreneurs, executives, middle-men and the like. On the face of it this latter group was obsessed with material advancement. Their principal bogeys were inflation, price increases and rent increases. By mid-1975 they were becoming uneasy on these counts, but they were still basically supporters of the regime. What other conceivable government in Iran would do as much for them as the Pahlavis had done?

Equally there were no signs of the well-known Middle Eastern ingredients for discontent amongst the armed forces, the foundation of the Shah's power. They were a privileged class, kept separate from the civilian population, well paid and protected from inflation by subsidies and fringe benefits. They were lavishly armed and equipped and constantly expanding. The Shah's foreign policies were thrusting enough to satisfy their vanity but not so rash as to put them in physical danger. They had every reason to remain united and loyal behind their Commander-in-Chief.

My general conclusion therefore was that the political and economic malaise of 1975 did not constitute a threat to the existence of the regime. Iran was a classic case of the rapid transformation of a traditional Middle Eastern society into a modern, developed state – or something approximating to one – under dynamic, authoritarian leadership. Most people were benefiting from the Shah's revolutionary policies. Certainly there was social upheaval, serious inflation, and rising expectations which could not be fully met. Negative, old-fashioned attributes persisted in the regime – despotism, corruption, nepotism, repression and brutality – which had alienated in particular the younger, educated generation. The traditional guardians of Iranian society, the mullahs and the bazaar, were hostile and apprehensive respectively. Hence the political malaise and the sporadic violence. But it was impossible to see how these disparate elements of opposition could combine to unseat a powerful and resolute monarch, buttressed by strong and united armed services. There was not, as I saw it, a revolutionary situation in the country.

The Shah was aware of the malaise, although he tended to attribute its causes to the machinations of foreigners; his own policies could not be misguided. His strategy was to accelerate the drive towards the Great Civilisation in order to render irrelevant the traditional sources of opposition (mainly the religious classes) and to neutralise his more modern opponents by a rising tide of economic activity and national prosperity. I have already mentioned some of the steps which he had taken to rationalise the worst excesses of the boom year and to combat the evils of inflation, corruption, waste and incompetence. Politically his reaction was a characteristic mixture of repression, misplaced experimentation and material inducement. The press was further muzzled and effectively reduced to a handful of slavish propaganda broadsheets. Discontented students were treated as enemies of the state and police violence was freely directed against them. SAVAK became even more ubiquitous and all the evils of a police state were intensified. These policies, apart from their effect on their immediate victims, probably did more to antagonise thinking people at all levels than anything else.

Alongside this brutal use of the stick, the Shah arbitrarily decided in March 1975 to abolish the multi-party system (which had degenerated into a farce) and to create in its place a single party of National Resurgence (Rastakhiz). This was to be a 'King's Party' to which all loyal Iranians should adhere – absurdly those who refused to join were to be formally offered their passports and a passage to exile. The objective was to mobilise the whole country, within the framework of Rastakhiz, behind the Shah's policies. Only constructive criticism would be allowed – even encouraged – and those who criticised from outside the party were to be labelled as traitors. This experiment, like so many previous ones, failed to gain momentum. There were of course massive public expressions of support and wholesale adherences to

16

Rastakhiz from institutions of all kinds throughout the country. Survivor techniques, always common in Iran, were widely practised, but there was no evidence of genuine popular enthusiasm, no belief that the Shah would allow Rastakhiz to evolve into an independent body which could offer a challenge to his authoritarianism, no sense that the new creation was more than another of the Shah's political gimmicks, doomed to inanition from the outset.

His material inducements were directed to the new class of industrial workers and were enshrined as a fresh stage in the Shah–People Revolution, the industrial equivalent of land reform. A decree was passed compelling all owners of manufacturing plants over a certain size to sell 49 per cent of their equity to their workers within a certain time limit; a greater share was to be sold to the workers in nationalised industries. This ploy also failed to have the desired impact. Given their innate sense of insecurity and lack of faith in authority, the workers showed a marked preference for holding on to their wages in cash and eschewed the option of share participation in spite of the generous terms offered. The net effect therefore was to create uncertainty and alarm amongst the industrialists and entrepreneurs, who began to show reluctance to invest additional capital in their businesses if it was likely to be put at risk by the Shah's arbitrary decisions, taken without any prior consultation with those who would be most affected.

My own belief, as expressed at the time, was that, if the Shah was to have any hope of eliminating the negative factors and stimulating on a large scale the genuine inspiration (as opposed to acquiescence and greed) which was necessary to achieve his dream of the total transformation of Iran, the key lay, not in trying to perpetuate a regimented society based on industrialisation, agricultural development and experimental political creations, but in his success in what might be described as the social and administrative sectors. If the long overdue crash programmes for universal medical care, for school and university expansion combined with qualitative improvement, for manpower training, for modernised distribution methods, for improved communications, for administrative reform, and for the elimination of corruption could be pressed forward vigorously, even at the expense of grandiose concepts such as nuclear power stations, the root causes of apathy and opposition might disappear, the dissidence might subside and hence the temptation towards repression. But I admitted that these were very big 'ifs', as they were in other countries in analogous situations.

I drew certain conclusions for Britain from the more uncertain situation in Iran in 1975. There was no doubt that the continuation of the Shah's regime and the achievement of his goals were in our interest. We would be unlikely to see another regime in Iran whose commercial, foreign and strategic policies would be more favourable to our own objectives and with which we could share so intimate a working relationship. But I did not believe that it would help for us to offer him advice on how to run his internal affairs, distasteful and counter-productive though some of his methods were. If we gave him advice to be more democratic, to ease up on the students, curb SAVAK, etc. we would only receive a whole colony of fleas in our ear and reduce our access to and influence with him. He had a long memory and the spectre of British interference in Iranian internal affairs was dormant, not dead. I rather believed that our best course, which would also be to our commercial and political advantage, would be to participate actively in those areas of social and administrative development to which I have drawn attention. These could form the foundations on which genuine stability might grow out of the political vacuum induced by strong, dictatorial government.

THREE

The Pahlavi Regime

It was the best of times, it was the worst of times; it was the
age of wisdom, it was the age of foolishness, it was the epoch
of belief, it was the epoch of incredulity, it was the season of
Light, it was the season of Darkness, it was the spring of hope,
it was the winter of despair.

Charles Dickens, *A Tale of Two Cities*

It is time that I examined in detail the nature of the regime in
whose permanence Britain had invested so much. Most of
the impressions with which I had set out for Tehran two
years previously had been confirmed by direct experience.
To all intents and purposes, the Shah was the regime: monarch and state had become virtually synonymous. The Shah
was at the centre of a series of circles, between which there
was little contact except through him – the Court, the Imperial Family, the central government, the system of provincial government, the armed forces, SAVAK and the police.
All these institutions functioned independently of each other
and each reported directly to the Shah. He was, for example,
the Chairman of the Higher Economic Council, comprising
the majority of the cabinet; the Commander-in-Chief of the
armed forces; the ultimate authority for the intelligence and
security apparatus; the immediate controller of the Court and
of the ramified activities which he had devolved to members
of his family.

What was he like, this man who had been brought to the
throne at the age of twenty-two under British and Soviet
occupation, who had reigned and ruled for over thirty years
through myriad political crises, who had survived several

assassination attempts and who now was the unquestioned dictator of his own country as well as a leading figure on the international scene?

By the end of 1975 I had established a close working relationship with him, having seen him alone or in company on an average of about once every two or three weeks over nearly two years. I still found him enigmatic, a compound of contrasts. His manner when faced with Western television interviewers was harsh, arrogant, patronising and didactic. His public utterances to his people were carefully prepared, flat and uninspired. In private he was quiet, reflective, remarkably well informed on foreign affairs and military matters, an attentive listener. Socially he was shy, withdrawn and devoid of small talk: a trivial question invariably received a serious and detailed answer. He despised and disliked intellectuals and ideologues – 'all these "isms"' – but had no doubt of his ability to translate his own elaborate theoretical concepts into practice. Intensely hard-working and devoted to the realisation of his dreams for Iran, he had few relaxations apart from physical exercise – he was an excellent rider, skier and tennis player.

As a maker of policy, he was a fascinating mixture of boldness, opportunism and caution. The visible manifestation of Iranian power and glory was a prominent element in his calculations, but he took few risks without taking out compensating insurance. He was the author of the great oil price increase of December 1973 but thereafter his foreign policy became increasingly aligned to the West, the principal sufferers from the price rise. He supported the Kurdish rebellion in Iraq when it was prospering and his propaganda machine trumpeted that the Iranian army could be at the gates of Baghdad in twenty-four hours. And yet, when Kurdish resistance collapsed in the winter of 1974 and he faced the prospect of open warfare with Iraq, he ditched the Kurds and concluded an agreement with his arch-enemies in Iraq, an agreement which was substantially beneficial to the Iranian national interest. He leant increasingly on the United States and Western Europe, but balanced this alignment with growing trade and industrial co-operation with the Soviet Union and Eastern Europe – further balanced by careful cultivation of China. In questions of foreign and strategic policy he was a shrewd operator, a bravura performer who commanded respect.

The truth was that these were the subjects in which he was most interested and best informed. He had consorted for years with world leaders, he read the foreign press voraciously, and in effect acted as his own Foreign Minister with all the resources of the Foreign Ministry daily available to him. In this area of the national life he was the reverse of isolated and out of touch. It was a pleasure to do business with him.

The same could not be said of the Shah in relation to the domestic affairs of Iran. It was obvious from the start of my mission that he was severely and dangerously isolated in the pomp and grandeur which has·traditionally surrounded the Persian monarch. The Imperial Court radiated a hard, meretricious glitter; the main function of its elaborate ritual and rigid protocol seemed to be to shield the monarch from direct contact with his people. Security was an additional factor contributing to his isolation. This was not unreasonable given the number of assassination attempts against the Shah since the 1940s, but it was impossible for him to have a genuine feel for his people when he was never allowed to drive through the streets or to mix with crowds, and when, even at public functions, he was separated from the populace by bullet-proof glass and travelled everywhere by aircraft or helicopter.

I was introduced to this aspect of life in Iran at an early stage. In May 1974 I accompanied the Shah on a visit to the new complex of agri-businesses in the south-west (they were all bankrupt a year or so later), one of which was partially owned and wholly managed by British interests. Elaborate security plans were discussed before the Shah's arrival and the programme had, to my surprise, been arranged in such a way that he would only meet the foreign management team, avoiding the hundreds of Iranian workers on the estate. To my delight, something went wrong and the Shah and I, with his immediate entourage, suddenly found ourselves engulfed by a milling crowd of shouting, gesticulating farm workers and technicians, bellowing speeches into the Shah's face and thrusting petitions under his nose. Used as I was to the cosy egalitarianism of the Arab world, I regarded this as a normal phenomenon and was interested to see how the Shah would react. He was entirely composed, smiling and responding as best he could to the confused roar of praise and requests which rose around us. Suddenly, out of the corner of my eye, I saw a company of infantry – there had been no soldiers in sight before – advancing on us at the double with fixed bayonets, obviously under orders to disperse the crowd by force. Fortunately the Shah's military ADC ordered them off and the moment of tension passed.

When we returned to our cars to drive to the spot at which the imperial helicopters were parked, I found myself sitting with Assadollah Alam, Minister of Court and unquestionably the most powerful man in the country after the Shah, of whom more hereafter. 'That was one of the worst moments of my life,' he said as we sank back on the cushions. I could not understand what he meant and said so. The little incident had seemed to me to be an admirable example of direct contact between Shah and people (after all were we not living in a Shah–People Revolution?) from which the Shah had emerged with credit, leaving the farmers with the warm feeling of having spoken man to man with their ruler. 'But the security risk was appalling,' replied Alam, 'and what would have happened if the soldiers had started shooting?' What indeed, I thought, realising that I had entered a very different world from that to which I had become accustomed elsewhere in the Middle East.

During the next year, I experienced many demonstrations of the Shah's remoteness from his people; in fact, during my five years in Iran, the unrehearsed scene at the Iran Shellcott agri-business was the only occasion on which I saw the Shah in spontaneous contact with his subjects. I noticed, again with initial surprise but later as a matter of course, that the presence of the populace at all major events attended by the Shah was a sham. At the opening of the Asian Games in the colossal Aryamehr Stadium in the summer of 1974, the crowd of 100,000 who greeted the Shah with well-drilled enthusiasm were in fact mainly drawn from units of the armed forces plus carefully selected delegations from the ruling political party, boy scouts, women's organisations and the like. The

annual military parade held in December to celebrate the
liberation of Azerbaijan from the Soviet Union and its pup-
pets in 1946 did not consist of a triumphal drive through the
streets of Tehran with the Shah on the saluting base surrounded by his people. It was held on a deserted stretch of
road some miles outside the capital. The Shah would arrive
in a helicopter, ride a horse for 200 yards and spend the
ensuing hours in a bullet-proof glass box built for the purpose. The small audience of shivering diplomats, Iranian
military and civil dignitaries and carefully chosen representatives of the people sat in open tin lean-to sheds while
the tanks and guns rumbled past, the aircraft zoomed over-
head and the troops goose-stepped briskly past their
Commander-in-Chief in his glass enclosure.

The propaganda machine went to Orwellian lengths to
sustain the myth of the Shah's mystical union with his people
and to disguise the reality of his remoteness. Television was
an invaluable aid to this deception. It was not until early 1976
that I realised what was happening. My wife and I were
attending the ceremonies at Reza Shah's mausoleum to com-
memorate the fiftieth anniversary of Pahlavi rule. The Shah
and the Empress arrived, as usual, by helicopter, landing
about 200 yards away from the mausoleum. We heard a short
burst of applause and, about two minutes later, the imperial
couple walked past us and mounted the steps of the mausoleum. The ceremonies took their course. When we left and
were driving back to Tehran I noticed to my astonishment
four horses' heads peering out of what looked like an enormous Black Maria. 'SAVAK have started arresting horses, it
seems,' I said to my wife. A little further on we passed a tank
transporter carrying a state coach wrapped in a large plastic
sheet. 'How odd,' I remarked, 'the Shah and the Empress
must have walked from the helicopter; it was only a hundred
yards or so.' When we got back to our house we watched the
whole ceremony on television. I was nonplussed to see the
Shah and Empress driving in an open coach drawn by horses
for what seemed many miles, flanked on both sides by cheer-
ing crowds! It was of course a sham: they must have driven
in the coach for about fifty yards between a small claque
before they walked up the steps of the mausoleum. But, for

the millions of television viewers, quite a different impression was created.

Amongst the diplomatic corps this kind of thing was the subject of laughter and mockery – an amalgam of Ruritania and *1984* – rather than concern. But, as I gained in experience, I became worried at the effect of this isolation on the Shah's own judgment. He heard the truth from foreigners about foreign policy matters and about Iran's performance as it affected foreign powers, and he did not shrink from it. I recall an occasion in 1975 when he asked me for an honest assessment of the performance of the Iranian brigade in Oman, adding, 'My generals tell me they are perfect, but you know the truth and I want to hear it.' I told him that, on a scale of ten, we would award them five marks: the senior officers were rigid and unimaginative; the troops tough but ill trained for guerilla warfare; their tactics at platoon and company level were poor; they refused to patrol at night; and so on. The Shah accepted this not particularly complimentary assessment of his beloved troops without blinking. I could quote many similar examples. But, on domestic matters where foreigners feared to tread, my belief was that he was only told what he wanted to hear, that his vaunted intelligence services were as bad in this regard as his ministerial technocrats and the sycophants of the Court, and that his isolation prevented him from gauging the temper of his people at first hand. Otherwise a man of his shrewdness and innate caution would surely not have permitted some of the senseless and pointless affronts to the Iranian tradition which disturbed many of us during my first two years. I do not believe that, if he had been better informed, he would have modified the unrealistic magnitude of the main development projects of the boom year, those projects which died in 1975 after contributing to the administrative, social and economic chaos of 1974. Nor would he have reduced his military programme, ambitious though it was in terms of equipment and manpower. These were central to his vision of Iran taking its place as a Western, industrialised, powerful, independent nation, on equal terms with the major powers of Western Europe. But would he have allowed the Empress to arrange a Zoroastrian Congress in Tehran in the middle of the fasting month of Ramadan, concluding with a champagne reception at the palace? Would he have permitted the avant-garde absurdities of the annual Shiraz International Cultural Festival? Would he have authorised the bulldozing of the ancient bazaar around the Holy Shrine at Mashhad, exposing the Shrine rather as a cathedral close exposes an English cathedral? It seemed to me – certainly to my Arab diplomatic colleagues who boycotted the reception at the close of the Zoroastrian Congress – that this kind of thing was liable to have a greater impact on the deeply religious Muslim masses and their dissident religious leaders than the failure of some grandiose economic projects amongst the genuine social and economic progress which the country was making. Perhaps he, or the Empress, saw these manifestations as a kind of shock treatment designed to galvanise the people of Iran out of their Islamic torpor. Perhaps they were done to impress foreigners with the cosmopolitanism and modernity of Iran – it was to be one of the centres of the world in cultural terms as well as in terms of political, military and industrial power. But the Shah should have known better. He disliked the religious classes – 'black reaction' – as much as he disliked the communists – 'red revolution' – or even more. Nevertheless he had not declared open war on them; he went through the Islamic motions himself and, at his orders, many leading religious dignitaries were in receipt of secret subventions. Why therefore offer gratuitous ammunition to those whom he knew to be opposed to him and fertilise the ground of dissent with no clear compensating gain? These were questions which worried me at the time, but I did not consider it part of my job to discuss them with the Shah.

I saw the Empress as the perfect complement to the Shah. Where he inspired awe and fear, she inspired love and affection. Beautiful, intelligent, artistic, compassionate, she seemed to have a remarkably free and open relationship with her husband. The general view was that she was one of the very few people who could speak their minds to him and that her influence was beneficial. She patronised intellectuals and artists and accomplished a great deal in terms of social welfare and charity, acting as an example and an inspiration to the Iranian upper establishment, not by nature conspicuous for their altruism. Not having been brought up in the purple under the aegis of a savage and domineering father, as was the case wíth the Shah, she was more open, more extrovert, more sensitive to the people. She resented the curbs of security and of administrative convenience and broke them wherever she could. I remember being told by a provincial governor how she had arranged to visit a certain village where, of course, everything had been carefully prepared for her. En route, she suddenly decided to visit another village where nothing had been prepared and where she would see the life of the villagers as it really was. The governor said that he was overcome by the demonstrations of real, spontaneous love with which she was greeted on this surprise visit. I too remember, in 1975, conducting her round the British pavilion at the annual International Trade Fair in Tehran. Again her visit was a surprise and the pavilion was swarming with Tehranis of the artisan class, men and women. I shall never forget the Empress's rage when her security guards started brutally to clear a way for her down one crowded alley and how she then plunged unguarded into the mass of people. There was no doubt of the sincerity of her reception.

She had a fine sense of the value of the Iranian artistic tradition and did much to prevent the juggernaut of the Great Civilisation from destroying all that was best in Iranian domestic architecture. Old houses, particularly in the provinces, were bought, restored and opened to the public. Iran-.ian paintings, ceramics and carpets were collected and displayed in new museums, sometimes in converted palaces. She encouraged Iranian music, theatre and intellectual life. Through her efforts, internal tourism increased with the mobility of rising prosperity, and middle-class Iranians began to take pride in the visual evidence of the greatness of their country's past.

All this, and more, was admirable and the Empress's activities did much to temper the gross materialism which was the principal manifestation of the Great Civilisation. I felt it a pity that the Empress's visions for Iran's cultural future, as opposed to her regard for all that was beautiful and valuable in its past, were too cosmopolitan, too avant-garde for the country to stomach. As I have mentioned, the political effect of the Shiraz Festival was serious and much of the Festival was unnecessarily devoted to the radical 'fringe' of the arts. Why also spend so much on European art collections, on grandiose cultural centres which were beyond the capacity of the country to operate?

And then there was Alam, Minister of Court, the man of power. Assadollah Alam came of an ancient, aristocratic family from Birjand in eastern Iran. The family's roots reached back through the centuries to the independent Tahirid dynasty of the tenth century and even further back to distinguished Sassanian and Arab origins. For many years the Alams had faithfully served the ruling dynasty. Assadollah's father had been close to Reza Shah and Assadollah himself had been a confidante and friend of Mohammed Reza Shah for as long as any of us could remember. He had held a variety of high offices and had been Prime Minister at the time of the Tehran bazaar riots of 1963. Alam had given the order for the troops to fire on the rioters; in his own words to me in 1975: 'I had to. His Majesty is very soft-hearted and does not like bloodshed.'

Shrewd, masterful and politically sensitive, Alam was probably the only person, apart from the Empress, who could speak frankly to the Shah, disagree with him and persuade him to change course. In his slightly old-fashioned, feudal way, he had a feel for the people, which was conspicuously lacking throughout the rest of the Pahlavi establishment. He could be tough and ruthless but he was well informed and the network of his political constituency was spread throughout the country. His family had for generations been Anglophiles, not for reasons of self-interest or subservience, but because they judged that friendship with Britain was in the best interests of Iran. He and I had become close friends and I leant on him heavily for advice and information. It was always well founded. Sadly, by the time I arrived in Tehran, he was already in the grip of leukaemia, the disease which killed him in early 1978. His brain was as active as ever but he tired easily. As he confessed to me many times, he was finding it increasingly difficult and costly in nervous energy to face down the Shah as the latter became more remote and fixed in his arrogant certainties. Alam's strategy was to let minor matters pass and to reserve his strength for crucial issues. But he remained without question the most powerful man in the country after the Shah and was deferred to by all including the Prime Minister. After two years I had formed a deep affection and respect for him, and, when things seemed to be going alarmingly wrong, was consoled by his steadying and sagacious presence.

The Imperial Family – the Shah's many sisters and brothers – were deployed in the area of the Court, each with responsibility for a quasi-independent para-statal organisation, independent of central government. Princess Ashraf, the Shah's twin sister, a formidable and energetic lady who frequently represented Iran in international organisations, was Head of the Imperial Organisation for Social Services; Princess Shams, the Shah's elder sister, ran the Iranian Red Crescent while the half-brothers had lesser areas of responsibility. Most of them, and their children, were charming and intelligent people and Princess Ashraf had an exceptionally strong and dynamic personality which led to frequent ill-feeling between her and the Shah. Politically the family was an albatross around the Shah's neck. A strong smell of corruption hung around them, particularly during the boom when the scale of kick-backs reached astronomical heights. True or false, the political reality was that everyone believed it was difficult, if not impossible, to secure contracts without the intervention of this prince or that princess. Specific rumours in support of this proposition were legion and each individual area of development came to be associated in the minds of the people with the depredations of Prince So-and-So or Princess Such-and-Such. Few members of the family, except the Shah, escaped this kind of accusation, thus providing plentiful ammunition for the dissidents. The luxurious way of life of the family compounded this evil and even the Shah's supporters complained that he did nothing to keep them under control. Of course I have no way of knowing the truth of these myriad stories of corruption and licence. Even if 10 per cent of them were true it would have been bad enough, but the important factor was not so much whether the accusations were justified, but that everyone believed them to be so.

Another para-statal organisation which played an important part in national life and was also the object of political obloquy was the Pahlavi Foundation. Again independent of central government, its tentacles reached out deep into many aspects of the economy, both at home and abroad. Originally established with its own bank (the Bank Omran) in order to put to good use the revenues from the sale of the Crown Lands, the Foundation invested in industry, hotels, real estate and services and allegedly devoted the profits to social services, to financing Iranian scholarships abroad and to other good works. It was impossible to discover exactly how it functioned and impossible to judge its ethical standard. No doubt it did some good and many people must have benefited from its activities. But, as with the Imperial Family, it was widely and cynically regarded as a corrupt organisation, a convenient slush fund for the Shah and the parasites surrounding him. This political reality was more important than the precise truth of the matter.

Next on the civilian side was the central government itself, by which I mean the cabinet and its ramifications such as the state development banks, the nationalised industries (oil, gas, electricity, etc.), the sum total of institutions which reported through the Prime Minister – although the Chairman of the National Iranian Oil Company discharged his responsibilities direct to the Shah. Never in my career had I encountered such a shining array of talent. With one or two exceptions the government establishment was composed of men of great skill, high intelligence and expertise and what seemed an infinite capacity for hard work. Many of them had spent years in the West as doctors, businessmen, bankers and academics. Some of them, notably Dr Jamshyd Amouzegar, Minister of Finance and subsequently Secretary-General of the Rastakhiz Party, had acquired international reputations. The Prime Minister, Amir Abbas Hoveyda, was a close friend of mine and I was unashamedly prejudiced in his favour. Sceptical, humorous, cultivated, he was the Sir Robert Walpole of Iran. For all his outward cynicism, he was a devoted patriot and a tireless worker for the good of his country.

They were all over-worked, harassed, and unable to delegate far down the bureaucratic line – the talent was thinly spread and had little depth. Perhaps the most striking feature of the government was its apolitical nature. They were technocrats in the true sense of the word. As Hoveyda put it to me, 'The Shah is the Chairman of the Board and I am the Managing Director.' He and his colleagues saw it as their patriotic duty to make the Shah's personal style of government work and to do everything they could to carry out his programmes. Yes, some of them were widely believed to be on the take, but the government's reputation as a whole was spotless compared to that of the Court and the Imperial Family. Hoveyda himself was beyond reproach, although, like Sir Robert Walpole, he was over-tolerant of the peccadilloes of others – 'to keep the boys happy'. They knew that they were all dependent for their jobs on the Shah's arbitrary whim and their brisk self-confidence evaporated quickly in the imperial presence. None of them was close to the Shah, not even Hoveyda who had been Prime Minister for twelve years by 1975, and I doubted whether, for all their misgivings, they dared to cross the Shah in his more extravagant moods; there was virtually no serious discussion when he decided at a stroke to double the fifth Five Year Plan, thus precipitating the chaos of the boom. Hoveyda's view as expressed to me was that they must do their best to get as much done as possible and that, however great the shortfall might be, a great deal would be achieved – as it was. He was in fact, together with the Mayor of Tehran, Gholamreza Nikpay, another close friend of mine, one of the few amongst the technocrats who had a political sense. He and the Mayor, although they disliked each other intensely, were adept at the politician's tricks of the trade, the rousing speeches at the (somewhat fascistic) political rallies, handshaking in the streets of Tehran, surprise visits to provincial towns, personal examinations of shops to see whether prices were fair, whistle-stop tours. Unlike most of their colleagues, some of whom seemed more American or European than Iranian, they had a sense of the temper of the people and I felt it a pity that the Shah should take so little account of their experience. Mayor Nikpay could have told him that the bizarre plan foisted on to the Minister of Commerce, Fereydoun Mahdavi, himself for many years resident in West Germany, to abolish the traditional system of small-scale bakeries and to convert the bread supply of Iran into sliced loaves on the Western model, was nonsense and would founder on the opposition of the multitude of small bakers in the bazaars. So it did, but only after considerable expenditure on feasibility studies and diversion of administrative manpower into the preparation of this abortive project. But, in the absence of serious collegiate discussion within the cabinet and between the cabinet and the Shah, the political ingredient was lost and much time and effort was wasted as these devoted men struggled unsuccessfully to fulfil their master's extravagant demands.

Lastly there were the twin foundations of Pahlavi power, the armed forces and SAVAK. Iran, unlike Turkey, was not a country with a tradition of a strong, regular army. By the mid-nineteenth century, the practice of levying feudal forces had fallen into decay and the rudimentary Persian army was ineffective. Centrifugal forces flourished and the writ of the central government was limited. The non-Persian provinces on the periphery of the Persian heartland - Azerbaijani Turks, Kurds, Arabs, Baluchis, Turcomen - had become nearly autonomous. The two dominant foreign powers - Britain and Czarist Russia - who had divided Iran into spheres of influence in 1907, were obliged to maintain security in their respective zones by raising their own forces, the Persian Cossacks commanded by Russian officers in the north, and the South Persia Rifles commanded by British officers of the Indian army in the south. As is well known, the Shah's father, then Reza Khan, was first a private and later an officer of the Persian Cossacks. Reza Khan was not unnaturally determined to eradicate a state of affairs in which the Iranian government could not even maintain its authority within its own borders, let alone protect itself from outside intervention. He resolved to create regular armed forces which would owe their primary loyalty to his regime and which would establish the rule of the Tehran government (or rather of the Pahlavi Shah) throughout the country, as well as demonstrating enough strength to deter any foreign aggressor. This creation of an indigenous military caste was an important innovation in the Iranian socio-political fabric but

Reza Shah's experiment, highly successful in establishing internal security and in reuniting the state under his rule, collapsed in the face of the Anglo-Soviet invasion of 1941. Mohammed Reza Shah set out to re-create and to augment his father's model. By 1975 he appeared to have succeeded beyond the imagination of the previous generation. In the early 1960s he had established his personal domination over the armed forces by nominating his own appointees to the top posts. He maintained his unchallenged position as Commander-in-Chief and guarded against any co-ordinated move by his generals to oust him, firstly by appointing a series of loyal and not very bright heads of the individual services, secondly by personally supervising appointments and promotions down to a low level, thirdly by physically separating the headquarters of each of the three services, and finally by acting as his own Chairman of the Chiefs of Staff. The army, air force and naval commanders never met except in the presence of the Shah, and the Iranian equivalent of the Chief of the Defence Staff was rightly named Chief of Staff to the Commander-in-Chief, which was precisely what he was. There was no civilian control over the armed forces. The Minister of War in the cabinet was a serving or retired general who carried out routine administrative functions, somewhat analogous to those of a Quarter-Master General.

The armed services were a privileged and pampered class. Deluged with modern and sophisticated equipment, they were kept quite separate from the civilian population. They were mainly conscripts but the senior NCOs, the bulk of the officers and all ranks of certain units of the Imperial Guard were regulars. Most large towns and cities had their garrisons, conspicuously sited on the outskirts: high-rise blocks of married quarters, discount shops, schools and sports facilities were familiar sights, evidence of the Shah's strategy of creating a distinct military caste which would not only give unquestioning loyalty to him and his successors but would also, as Reza Shah would have wished, terrify his foes both inside and outside Iran. Certainly the armed forces made a brave show. A few of the senior officers, not too many, were competent and intelligent: the British training and commissioning teams with the armoured regiments, the Junior Leaders Battalion, the navy and marines were fairly favourably impressed. But the top brass were mainly distinguished by their chestfuls of medals (from what wars, we wondered?) and by their Germano-American strutting. Particularly in the ground forces, boneheaded stupidity was not uncommon in the higher ranks; they were an arrogant lot. The rank and file, Central Asian peasants, looked tough and uncomplaining and the navy and air force were full of swagger and elan. The armed services were not popular amongst the civilian population; their high-handed behaviour in the streets and the shops (which I have already mentioned), their favoured position, their possession of the lion's share of the budget, guaranteed that. But, superficially at least, they appeared to constitute a formidable platform for the regime to rest on.

Finally there was SAVAK which, by the mid-1970s, had become one of the principal bogeys of the Western press and of human rights activists in Europe and the United States. Was this organisation as bad as it was painted? Probably, but one must add that similar atrocities were no doubt carried out by other secret police forces in many Third World dictatorships. The head of SAVAK, General Nematollah Nassiri, was not a subtle operator. He was an unintelligent, devotedly loyal, former Commander of the Imperial Guard, a brave man who had personally delivered to Dr Mossadegh the Shah's dismissal of him as Prime Minister; he was arrested for his pains and was lucky to have escaped with his life. He was a callous man and would have sanctioned any action in support of the Pahlavis. Indiscriminate harassment and brutality rather than sophisticated counter-subversion was SAVAK's style under Nassiri. Mass arrests were common and SAVAK was believed to have permeated all important sectors of the national life, government, universities, factories, Iranian student organisations overseas, and the political parties (such as they were). This reputation for ubiquitousness was carefully cultivated and, for simple reasons of manpower, it seemed improbable that SAVAK could actually be as all-seeing as folklore would have it. My own conclusion, necessarily tentative because of the lack of hard evidence, was that too much attention was paid to communists and other left-wing groups, to the student body as a whole and to surveillance of Iran's known friends such as ourselves: it was a source of amusement to us that the cigarette kiosk immediately outside the Embassy gates contained a radio-telephone. I used to wonder whether SAVAK ever asked themselves why dissidence was so widespread or whether they confined themselves to savage attacks on the symptoms of dissidence. In this context I remember mentioning to the Shah some time in 1975 how appalled I had been by the atmosphere on the many university campuses which I had visited. Even a foreign Ambassador on a carefully stage-managed visit could not but be aware of the sullenness and hostility of the students, not to speak of the visible evidence of police and SAVAK surveillance. 'It is only a small handful of foreign-inspired troublemakers,' was the reply. 'They have to be dealt with firmly.' At the time I assumed that this was an indirect way of telling me to mind my own business: I assumed that the Shah must be aware of the extent and causes of student alienation. Now I wonder. Did he believe what he told me? Was his view based on General Nassiri's reports and, if so, was this what Nassiri himself believed?

What I have written in this chapter represents, as faithfully as memory permits, my own perception of the nature of the regime as I saw it after about two years in Iran. It was a comprehensive mixture of the admirable, the distasteful, the serious, the absurd. Propaganda far outran achievement and overt political activity was stifled by the Shah's repressiveness. He seemed to see himself as a combination of a tough battalion commander and a headmaster of a Victorian public school. Corruption was rife - it was the age of the middle-man - but there was also integrity and patriotic devotion. Substantial progress was vitiated by expensive failures. But, as I saw it, whatever the failings of the regime, weakness and indecision were not amongst them, and the armed might of the country solidly buttressed the monarch and his apparatus of state. So long as the armed forces remained loyal and united, and so long as economic and social progress continued, however haltingly, the risk of a sudden change of regime

seemed small, for all the fringe terrorism, the student dissidence, and the sullen hostility of the traditional classes of the
religious establishment and the bazaar. Thus I saw the picture as 1975 gave way to 1976, the year in which fifty years of
Pahlavi rule were due to be celebrated.

FOUR

The Embassy

Before addressing the evolving drama of the last three years of the Shah, it might be pertinent to say something of the organisation of the Embassy and of the associated governmental and semi-governmental British organisations in Iran. The emphasis which we placed on different aspects of our work is relevant to the whole analysis, indeed to our ability to answer accurately in our own minds and in our reporting the questions which we were continually asking ourselves about the strengths and weaknesses of Pahlavi-ism.

Anyone who has taken the trouble to read this far will have noticed a preponderance of the first person singular in the formulation of our views. This is not purely egoism – indeed the dénouement of this book would justify a different approach from the point of view of my self-esteem. I was the Ambassador and the ultimate responsibility for the assessments of the Embassy was mine; moreover I was also the most experienced Middle East specialist on the staff. I did not, however, run the Embassy as the Shah ran his government, neither seeking opinions from others nor being prepared to listen to views which did not coincide with my own. Some despatches and important telegrams I wrote myself and then sought the views of my senior staff before they were finalised. Others were prepared by my political or commercial staff, depending on the subject matter, and went through a wide process of consultation before reaching me in near final form. Alongside these bureaucratic procedures, there was continuous discussion ranging from formal weekly staff meetings to small ad hoc groups whose task was to consider individual questions. Hence the views which I have already expressed in previous chapters, although ultimately my own, represent a consensus of the Embassy view at the time.

By the end of 1975 I had, with the approval of the Foreign Office, reorganised the Embassy staff to meet our priorities. First came export promotion in all its aspects – dealing with the flood of business visitors and commercial enquiries, helping to organise trade promotions and trade delegations, seeking new commercial opportunities and feeding them into the export promotion machine back home. An analogous activity was keeping a close eye on Iranian oil and natural gas policy, the encouragement of Iranian inward investment in the United Kingdom, assisting British firms to establish Irano-British joint ventures in manufacturing and services, promoting the establishment of an Irano-British Chamber of Commerce, advising on the proposed Iranian financial projects such as the establishment of Tehran as an international financial centre, the expansion of the Tehran stock exchange – I could continue the list indefinitely. Suffice it to say that, in such a rapidly growing and complex market, there was enough work in this field to occupy the time of the whole Embassy staff, including myself. I therefore strengthened the commercial and economic section by the addition of extra personnel at desk level and by delegating the main responsibility for our export promotion and economic reporting activities to my (promoted) deputy, who had previously been involved solely on the political side. I was fortunate in this regard in having as my minister George Chalmers, one of the most knowledgeable and experienced officers in the service on commercial, economic, financial and oil matters.

So the core of the Embassy became the commercial section. Even the service attachés, of whom I had the full range covering the navy, the army and the air force, were primarily occupied not in the collection of military information about the Iranian armed forces, but in servicing our defence sales programme to Iran as well as assisting the British military training teams and the teams which were present to commission the new equipment which the Iranians were purchasing from Britain. Again the principal task of the service attachés was commercial, not political.

With the limitations on manpower which afflict all government departments in most countries, this left me with a relatively small political section. To be fair, Iran was so important to Britain that, had I made a case for political reinforcements, I would probably have got them; all my requests for expansion of the commercial section of the Embassy were met, notwithstanding the pressures on public expenditure in Britain in the 1970s. The fact is that, rightly or wrongly, I was satisfied with what I had.

The Chancery comprised a number (not large) of senior and junior officers, including two or three Persian speakers. They were expected to advise and report on the internal political situation as well as to conduct the large volume of routine business which we had with the Iranian Foreign Ministry and other government departments at working level. These included liaison with SAVAK, the police and with Iranian military intelligence. But this was in the context, partly under the CENTO umbrella, of the external threat to Iran, external subversion and threats to the stability of neighbouring states which were politically or strategically important to Iranian and British interests. In addition I had a press officer to deal with the local media and with foreign correspondents who also had a watching brief over domestic developments, and there were officers dealing with consular and cultural affairs.

I made the point in the earlier chapters that it was one of the cardinal elements of my policy to normalise relations with the Shah and his government and, by the same token, to lay the ghost of British interference in Iranian internal affairs. I therefore went out of my way not to use a number of obvious British sources for information gathering. By late 1975 there was a large British community scattered throughout Iran, perhaps as many as 15,000 to 20,000 people in all. We had British Council centres in Tehran, Shiraz, Ahwaz, Mashhad and Tabriz. Their main function was the teaching of English and liaison with the local universities, most of which had British lecturers on the staff. There were military teams and defence-related civilians in Tehran, Shiraz, Ahwaz, Bushire, Bandar Abbas and near the Caspian coast. They were engaged in training units of the Iranian armed forces, and commissioning and servicing British defence equipment. There were perhaps fifteen to twenty Irano-British manufacturing and service joint ventures in Tehran and the provinces, involved in the assembly or manufacture of a wide variety of products from motor cars to rubber gloves. British contractors were building power stations, naval and military technical installations, ports and workshops, housing complexes and much besides. In Tehran there was a thriving community of bankers, entrepreneurs, teachers, accountants, businessmen, etc. I and my staff had ample reason to travel throughout the country to visit the British communities in the provinces – sometimes a large project employing hundreds in or near a main city, sometimes a handful of technicians helping to open up a mine far down a dust road in a lonely range of hills, sometimes a missionary and his family in a Kurdish village, sometimes a military team in an isolated army garrison, sometimes a group of archaeologists working on a Median site; there was no lack of variety and I for one took full advantage of the opportunities to travel in this beautiful, vast, historically and archaeologically fascinating country.

But we did not use these people as 'agents' in the technical sense of the word. Of course we were interested to hear what they had to say about local conditions and of course we knew what questions to ask and what areas of conversation to develop, as we did with all our many Iranian contacts; but there was nothing covert or sinister about this. Not surprisingly in the light of their history, all Iranian regimes are secretive and suspicious of foreigners. This, as I wrote in my introductory chapter, applied in full measure to the British, for reasons which I have explained. I was not a victim of my own imagination. Even the presence of fluent Persian speakers on the Embassy staff was regarded not as a compliment to Iran, but as evidence of some sinister intent. On one occasion, the Ministry of Defence posted to our Chieftain tank commissioning team an officer who, fortuitously, was fluent in Persian. This would have seemed an obvious posting for an officer who also had the appropriate technical qualifications. Far from being welcome, the unfortunate officer was declared *persona non grata* as soon as the authorities discovered that he possessed this dangerous skill. I myself was made aware from the outset that my knowledge of Turkish was a liability rather than an asset (was I suspected of having a brief to encourage separatism in Turkish-speaking Azerbaijan?) and that my long experience in the Arab world (I was the first Diplomatic Service Arabist to be appointed Ambassador to Tehran) laid me open to the accusation of not being a 'friend of Iran'.

Hence the Embassy was primarily organised as an agency for the promotion of British exports and for the general commercial, financial and economic interests of Britain. This was true both of the civilian and the military staff while even the political officers had a brief to be on the lookout for fresh export opportunities. Even the British Council, although not at the expense of its purely cultural activities, was organised to concentrate on the commercial aspects of English language teaching and the promotion of the sale of British educational goods and services, such as a vigorous campaign to place Iranian students in British schools, universities and technical establishments, the creation in Iran of an equivalent to the British Open University, exchanges of university lecturers and so forth. Study of the internal political situation in Iran was an important, but subsidiary activity: important because we needed to report accurately to London and to give sound advice to potential British exporters and investors; subsidiary because of the discretion required in the collection of information and because, in my judgment, a major effort would only endanger our relationship with the regime without providing compensating advantages in terms of additional information beyond what we could acquire by open observation and the use of our experience and analytical powers.

FIVE

1976–1977

Even the English, who had the lessons of their own past to guide them, ... watched the gradual advance of this epoch-making revolution as if through a thick veil.

De Tocqueville, *The Old Regime and the French Revolution*

The country obediently went through the motions of celebrating fifty years of Pahlavi rule, but there was no trace of spontaneity or affection amongst the people; only some of the leaders of the armed forces appeared genuinely moved at the main ceremony at Reza Shah's mausoleum, a cold and magnificent occasion at a cold and magnificent place.

It was not a year for rejoicing. In March the Prime Minister confessed to the visiting British Foreign Secretary, Mr Callaghan, that the Iranian government had suffered from excessive euphoria in the boom of 1974 and early 1975. They had sacrificed financial prudence and rational planning for speed and execution on a grand scale. In future there would be greater circumspection and closer scrutiny of projects. This reflected the Shah's mood, for while two years of an economic performance with few encouraging peaks and a greater number of dispiriting troughs had given an even livelier sense of urgency to the Shah's thinking, his priorities were now more strictly ordered. The development budget under preparation for the sixth Five Year Plan would be focused more narrowly, on infrastructure both physical and human, on basic industry, on creating a larger role for the private sector. He would put the accent not on the confident belief that money, if spent in large enough quantities, could solve all problems, but on hard work, increased productivity, avoidance of waste and cost consciousness. There would be no fresh projects. Consolidation and reappraisal were the watchwords.

As, in June 1976, we reviewed Iran's progress towards the fulfilment of the fresh targets set for the fifth Five Year Plan in August 1974, the need for such sobriety was evident. Industrial growth had been impressive although it had lagged behind the targets set for it. Elsewhere it was hard to detect a relationship between promise and performance. Agriculture was a disaster and the government's assertion of a growth rate of 7 per cent a year a lie. Food imports were rising rapidly as demand increased, while agricultural production was probably falling as the villagers sold their land for real estate and industrial development and then flocked to the towns. Development of water resources was going well but communications infrastructure was a catastrophe. Port expansion had scarcely taken place and the extension of road and rail links amounted to about 20 per cent of the target figure. In the social field, there was a shortfall of nearly 90 per cent in the numbers scheduled to be undergoing technical training; education was expanding fast but the shortage of teachers was crippling; considerable progress was being made towards establishing universal free education, and good work had been done in bringing literacy programmes to rural and tribal areas; but all these programmes, including university expansion, had to suffer cutbacks for reasons of finance and shortages of trained personnel. The same was true in the health field. Iran had only 11,000 doctors in the country (an equivalent number was working abroad in lucrative practices in Western Europe and the United States) against a requirement for about 40,000–50,000. Of the existing 11,000 at least half were working in Tehran where they could line their pockets from private practice. Nursing and technical medical staff were scarce and training programmes could not produce instant results. Great efforts had been made to extend social insurance benefits to larger numbers of the population – they were, in the early 1970s, virtually confined to organised labour and government employees – but here again financial and administrative problems had seriously hampered progress.

It was in our judgment the relative lack of success of these social programmes which was likely to be most critical for the regime in the longer term. Progress towards a welfare state had been a central element in the Shah's 'white revolution'. This had been partly for idealistic reasons, partly in order to bypass the traditional centres of power and patronage and to establish a popular base for his dynasty; the Pahlavis were to be the rulers who had brought health, education and personal security to all the people of Iran where no Shah, landowner, plutocrat, mullah or ideologue had done so before.

It was not that he had failed. Given the appalling backwardness of Iran in the 1950s compared to any of its neighbours (with the exception of Afghanistan), enormous strides had been made. But it was noticeable in 1976 that higher wages and expectations were tending to make the urban working classes, particularly industrial and construction workers, more rather than less volatile in their political and social attitudes. The wide gap which the boom had opened between rural and urban incomes was acting as a powerful stimulus to the drift from countryside to towns, which was taking place at an unhealthy rate. The lack of urban housing was becoming an acute political problem. The Shah's laudable attempts to establish a welfare state were being vitiated by these and other factors, and rising expectations, fuelled by boastful and mendacious government propaganda, looked as though they would continue to outrun achievement, great though this had been.

There were some encouraging indications in this period of reappraisal. Hitherto the Shah's style had been that of the old-fashioned, autocratic company boss in his management of the economy. As the boom petered out, he became aware that the economy had become too large and too complex to be run by him as the sole Chairman. I noticed by the end of the year that there was far more genuine consultation and free debate on operational matters between him and his government than there had been two or three years previously.

Politically there were no signs that the situation was deteriorating; indeed there were vestigial signs of improvement. The Rastakhiz Party was still regarded with unqualified cynicism by the Tehran intelligentsia, but I gained the impression that the Shah was making a serious attempt to breathe life into it, albeit within carefully defined limits. The elections to the new Majles, under the single party system, in mid-1975 had been relatively open and, in 1976, there were many new faces in the parliament – skilled workers, farmers, members of the newly educated lower middle class. At a local level in the provinces, I saw evidence that the Rastakhiz Party was in certain areas becoming an effective ginger group which officialdom could not ignore. Jamshyd Amouzegar had been appointed Secretary-General of the Party in October 1975. He had no political constituency of his own but was regarded as an independently minded man, less tainted by subservience to the Shah than most of his technocratic colleagues, as well as being highly intelligent and competent. He told me that the Shah had given him fifteen years in which to turn Rastakhiz into a popular base to fill the vacuum after the Shah's departure from the scene. There was certainly no evidence that Rastakhiz was being allowed to become an effective instrument to control central government activity, still less participate in decision-making. Even so, at the end of 1976, I felt fractionally – I emphasise fractionally – less dismissive of Rastakhiz than I had been at its creation nearly two years before.

Equally, as I got to know more Iranians intimately, I realised that Iran was not a police state in the absolute and all-pervasive sense that we associate with European totalitarianism. In private, and in particular with foreigners, educated Iranians were persistently and devastatingly critical, not of the Shah's aims, but of the ineffectiveness of the authorities in trying to achieve them. These criticisms were voiced, so far as I could judge, more or less irrespective of who might be listening. This freedom of speech was some kind of safety valve to compensate for the absence of democratic institutions. Another was the freedom to travel abroad and to export money – there was no exchange control. By mid-1976 we believed that as much as $1 billion a month in private capital was being transferred abroad. This was of course bad for the economy and an indicator of political and economic insecurity. And yet it was a comfort to the monied classes to be able to travel, to own property in Europe and America, to be able to take a break from the claustrophobic climate of Pahlavi Iran. This was a freedom which citizens of communist countries might well have envied.

The affluent classes were doing well enough and their criticisms had a parlour ring. They, like all Iranians, were used to secret police, lack of freedom, insecurity. They, like all Iranians, were naturally cynical about authority but accepted that it was there, that it was as it was and that power and influence were more potent forces than institutionalised checks and rights. They, like all Iranians, were used to concentrating on self-interest, reluctant to commit themselves deep down to support any regime.

The problems lay lower down but even these seemed manageable. Materially the Shah had managed to deliver only small returns on vast expenditure. The burgeoning student body did not as a whole have the resources to hedge their bets with the ownership of property in London or Los Angeles, with or without a Swiss bank account. If their aspirations in Iran could not be better satisfied, they would become a serious source of disaffection.

The extremist groups, drawn as they were from the student class, had changed their tactics since 1975. They had gone underground to undermine the regime. Their open challenge to the security forces had failed and they had suffered heavy casualties, with perhaps as many as 250 killed in 1976. This was a quiet year, certainly in comparison with 1975, on the university campuses.

On the right, we had not altered our judgment that the element in the religious leadership which stood for religious purity and against modernisation still enjoyed a great deal of emotional support from the uneducated. We did not ignore their capacity to command popular support. I did not however expect them to take the initiative in challenging the regime, but rather to re-emerge as a potent source of fuel for active opposition if it developed.

My summing up at the end of the year ran roughly as follows. Iran was still enveloped in a miasma of uncertainty and malaise in the aftermath of the boom. In the short term governmental policies were likely to be more sober, more rational. The newly created single party seemed to be making a little headway. It had not been a bad year for the security services in their war with the terrorists and the country had on the whole been quiet. Certainly the internal situation was no worse, perhaps marginally better, and the atmosphere was a trifle less oppressive. But inflation was still hitting all classes of society hard, exaggerated expectations had not been met, and social conditions in the poorer areas of the great cities were bad. There was an immense problem facing the Shah of changing fundamental Iranian attitudes. However, although active discontent was probably running at a higher level amongst most elements of society than in the years before the boom, manifestations of discontent were likely to remain diffuse and without central leadership. There was not a revolutionary situation. The armed forces were loyal and, against this loyalty, no powerful basis of opposition to the regime stood much chance of coming into being. The danger was not so much the emergence of a revolutionary situation in the short term with the consequent collapse of Iranian 'stability'; it was more a question of whether the Shah would succeed in transforming Iran into a modern, industrialised state (or something approximating to one) without disrupting Iranian society to a point where his son would find it difficult to establish himself. His son would not have the experience and authority to dominate the armed forces that his father possessed and it was not easy to see how the Shah's policies would succeed in creating a broad enough popular base for his son to rely on. Nevertheless, for the moment, I saw no reason why we should not continue to pursue our major economic and commercial interests in Iran with all the vigour at our disposal. In spite of all the problems, the frustrations, the infuriating muddles, the delays, Iran was developing at a great rate; it was politically tranquil (by regional standards) and the government was well disposed. The economy was settling down to a slower and healthier rhythm. Much had been achieved and there seemed to me to be plenty more achievement to come.

For nearly a decade the Shah had enjoyed an exceptional relationship with the administration in Washington. First

President Nixon and after him President Ford had shown an unqualified confidence in the Shah which the latter had sought but not found from successive American Presidents throughout his reign. The Nixon/Ford era vindicated the Shah's strategy of trying to turn Iran into an independent but indispensable friend and ally of the most powerful state in the world. Following Nixon's visit to Iran in 1972 (two American colonels were assassinated in Tehran shortly before the President's arrival), the Shah received political carte blanche to purchase any American military equipment which he wanted, short of nuclear weapons. With British disengagement from the Persian Gulf at the end of 1971, Nixon had conferred on the Shah the accolade of making him and his country one of the first exemplars of the Nixon doctrine of devolving strategic responsibility, which would otherwise have to be assumed by the United States, to powerful regional states. Iran was to constitute the main force for stability in the Persian Gulf and its hinterland, thus forming a first line of defence for the crucial Western interest in the oil of the Gulf and Saudi Arabia. This enhanced status for the Shah in American eyes created an unique nexus of interdependence. The Shah adopted foreign and strategic policies which suited the United States (and Britain for that matter); in return, the cornucopia of American arms supplies and political support was opened wide. The Shah lamented the fall of President Nixon but, by that time, his ties with the Republican Party ran wide and deep and he could be confident that Gerald Ford, no innovator, would not change course. Nor did he.

The Shah made no secret of his apprehension at the victory of President Carter in the elections of November 1976. He had never been comfortable with Democrat Presidents, who were more disposed than their Republican counterparts to inject a moralising element into the formulation of American foreign policy. The calculating opportunism of Nixon and Kissinger was far more to the Shah's taste. President Carter's vigorous public espousal of the cause of human rights in Third World countries, including Iran, and his emphasis on the need to reduce the volume of transfers of military equipment to the Third World, did nothing to allay the Shah's fears. A period of uncertainty in Irano-American relations ensued. Needless to say the reaction of the Shah's opponents, particularly the large and vociferous student community in the United States and the *ci-devant* political leaders in Tehran (whose fortunes had briefly prospered in President Kennedy's day), was precisely the reverse. They took comfort and courage from what they rightly detected as a potential weakening of the absolute support which their enemy had received from Washington for so many years.

In retrospect it is astonishing that the Shah should have chosen this moment to initiate a perceptible liberalisation of his regime. Many people argued at the time and subsequently that this liberalisation was the direct result of pressure from the Carter administration. To put it crudely, President Carter had told the Shah that, if the human rights situation in Iran was not improved and if a start was not made towards a freer, more democratic political structure, he could no longer rely on American material and moral support. I do not know the truth but I did not accept this theory then and I do not now. In fact the first, faint glimmers of liberalisation were discernible in late 1976, two or three months before President Carter's inauguration. I have no doubt that the Shah, with his usual opportunism, appreciated that a more humane and democratic attitude on his part would endear him to the new President and deflate American pressure which would otherwise build up against him; but I do not believe that this was his primary motive. I have never fully understood why, in terms of his own survival, so shrewd a man as the Shah should have chosen a time to liberalise when his economic and social promises to the people had fallen far short of fulfilment, when the political and social morale of the population as a whole was depressed, when the regime seemed to everyone to have lost the initiative in its bid for the total transformation of Iranian society, when the bright horizons of which the Shah had boasted as being near at hand were receding far beyond reach. A less propitious time for a loosening of political control could scarcely be imagined.

My tentative view then, and I have not revised it with hindsight, was that the Shah's decision was based on the following factors. In 1976, he had been talking more frequently in private about voluntary abdication. His idea was that he should step aside, perhaps in the mid-1980s, in favour of his son while he himself was still capable of exercising a controlling and stabilising influence behind the scenes during the difficult period of transition. He was aware that his own power was narrowly based, resting as it did on the loyalty of the armed forces and security services. This would not do for his son and for the perpetuation of the Pahlavi dynasty. He had tried to create a broader political base with the Rastakhiz Party but it had failed to get off the ground, and did not look like rising above the parish pump level of local politics. Time was beginning to press on the Shah (in retrospect he must have had his own illness much on his mind) and he needed to take a fresh political initiative in order to secure his son's heritage. He had tried in turn direct rule, a multi-party system, and a single party: none had succeeded. Why not therefore slacken the reins and see what happened? Perhaps some acceptable political pattern might emerge spontaneously without direction from on high. Such a policy would carry with it the bonus of pleasing the new and uncertain American President as well as deflecting mounting criticism in Western Europe. If it worked, well and good. If it did not, then it would not be difficult to pull in the reins again (such was the Shah's confidence in his ability to manipulate the internal political scenery according to his wishes).

As was normal in the secretive world of Iran, nothing was said publicly by the government. But, as 1976 turned to 1977, it became noticeable that, by the rigorous standards of the previous few years, there was a new atmosphere of greater political freedom, as well as improved treatment of those opposed to the regime. About 1,000 prisoners were amnestied in batches on appropriate occasions such as the Persian New Year and the Shah's birthday – including a large number of political detainees. For the first time for some years an open trial was held of people accused of anti-state activities, and foreign observers were allowed to witness the court proceedings. The International Committee of the Red Cross was authorised to inspect Iranian prisons. A new law was enacted forbidding detention without trial. Alongside these concrete measures, greater public freedom of expression was allowed. The newspapers became a little less slavish and a little more readable. Cyclostyled letters began to circulate, signed openly by lawyers, writers, academics, and members of the old National Front political parties. These letters were severely critical of the policies and performance of the regime and suggested remedies. Nothing happened to the authors and, in turn, the sermons from the Friday mosques became more strident and overtly hostile to the Shah's policies of modernisation, and even to the dynasty itself. Again there were no arrests, no acts of retaliation by the authorities, at least for the first ten months or so of the year.

These faint breaths of political fresh air were not matched by any improvement in the economic situation. The after-effects of the boom seemed to be beyond correction. Inflation was again running very high, perhaps around 30 per cent a year, a worse figure than that for 1975 or 1976. The government's projects for low cost urban housing, particularly in Tehran, had collapsed and been abandoned. The conditions of the poor in south Tehran had become scandalous. Then, in the summer, the national electricity grid gave way under the weight of expanded industrial and domestic demand. There was an acute shortage of electric power in towns and cities, leading to industrial damage and domestic distress. As always, the richer areas of Tehran suffered the least and the lights of north Tehran were clearly visible to the inhabitants of the poorer southern quarters as they sweltered, sometimes for days, without light, air-conditioning or refrigerators – boons which the drive to the Great Civilisation had only too recently brought to them.

Conditions in the provinces were less acute and, as I travelled, I was impressed by the cleanliness, prosperity and bustle of the medium-sized provincial towns, whether on the rim of the Great Eastern Desert, in Kurdestan, Azerbaijan, or Lurestan. There was no question but that life at all levels in the provinces was improving and that this improvement was taking place without the concomitant of that violent disruption of socio-economic conditions so evident in the neurotic, teeming, grimy streets and bazaars of Tehran. In towns as distant from each other as Semnan on the edge of the Eastern Desert and Khorramabad, capital of Lurestan in western Iran, it seemed to me as though a fairly happy process of transition was under way, with the new complementing the best of the old, not trampling it into the dust.

Even as the economy continued to falter, I took some comfort from the more open atmosphere which prevailed in the first half of 1977. It was refreshing to hear young Iranians – I am thinking in particular of archaeologists and social workers with whom I stayed on provincial tours – expressing strongly critical views, admitting past mistakes, and debating how the affairs of the country could and should be better conducted in the future. It was a relief to hear ministers, factory managers and industrial entrepreneurs making no bones about the difficulties they were experiencing with shortages of labour, the power generation crisis, with overproduction of certain products for markets which had not materialised, with high unit costs and poor quality control. This was a welcome change from the braggadocio of earlier years, the arrogant confidence that all would be well if Iran continued to expand, the bogus M.I.T. theorising and dreamlike statistical constructs. I began to feel that this new realism must be a healthy development and that, if combined with greater political freedom to participate in the running of the country, if only through the freedom to criticise, Iran might be about to enter a more stable and orderly phase of progress, as opposed to the hectic frenzies of the boom and the malaise which followed its end.

The Shah dramatised the advent of this new era by forcing the resignation of Amir Abbas Hoveyda in August and replacing him as Prime Minister by Dr Jamshyd Amouzegar. Hoveyda had been Prime Minister for thirteen years and had come to epitomise all that was expansive and optimistic in governmental policy. He had also come to symbolise a deliberate policy of subordinating the authority of the cabinet, and indeed of the whole political system, to the authority of the Shah, of turning the government into the Shah's personal management team. The contrast with Amouzegar was vivid. The latter was brilliantly clever and able – as was Hoveyda – and had retained a reputation, even amongst opponents of the regime, for having maintained more independence of mind than the remainder of his cabinet colleagues. Economically he made clear from the outset that he would adopt an austere, prudent, Treasury type of policy, the antithesis of the free-spending Hoveyda years.

And Alam, too, resigned from the post of Minister of Court. He went for genuine reasons of ill-health. He was dying (he was dead by early 1978) and could do no more, for all his devotion and strength of character. The Shah had lost one of his very few trusted friends, about the only man who could and did stand up to him and tell him the truth. Hoveyda replaced Alam but, notwithstanding his skill and experience, no one believed that he would acquire a comparable intimacy with the Shah. His appointment was regarded more as a consolation prize for losing the Prime Ministry than a promotion, and many people felt that the Shah had made a tactical error in not sweeping Hoveyda clear out of the governmental establishment: his retention of office had clouded the clarity of the break with the past which the Shah was trying to demonstrate to the country.

By the early autumn the political atmosphere was more vibrant than at any time since I had arrived in Tehran in early 1974. But there were no serious signs of incipient anarchy or loss of governmental control. To illustrate this point, we had no hesitation in continuing with plans to stage the longest, largest and most comprehensive British Cultural Festival which Britain had ever mounted overseas. The Festival, which was backed by funds from the British Council, the Iranian government and the British private sector, was an attempt to show to the people of Iran that Britain had a great deal more to offer than an imperial past and a present hunger for lucrative contracts. The regime supported it with enthusiasm and Princess Fatemeh, the Shah's youngest half-sister, was a vigorous and competent President of the Organising Committee. The Festival took place over a period of three weeks from October 4th to 24th. British military bands in full uniform played in the public parks of Tehran and in stadiums in the provinces; the Royal Ballet, the Prospect Theatre Company, the Aeolian String Quartet and others performed in Tehran; there was a wide series of exhibitions in the capital and in the provinces; and much more. Audiences were enthusiastic, security precautions in public places negligible, and there was no evidence of resentment or hostility. On the contrary, the whole exercise was an unqualified success and we congratulated ourselves that we had fulfilled our objectives. Even six months later anything of the kind would have been unthinkable.

Nevertheless, we were conscious in the last few months of the year that the Shah was grossly mishandling the new political situation which he had allowed to develop. By permitting greater freedom of expression he had in effect invited his people to open a dialogue with his regime. But when they did so by means of the open letters which were signed, not by communists or radicals of the right or left, but by respectable and respected members of the Iranian academic and professional establishment, they at first received no response – their reasoned criticisms of government policy were simply ignored. Then, in the late autumn, the newly active political groups were physically attacked and beaten up by 'spontaneous patriotic elements' and mysterious bomb explosions took place in the offices of people who had dared to criticise the regime. Peaceful demonstrations and meetings were broken up by club-swinging thugs, and individuals, including women, were waylaid and beaten on their way to or from political meetings.

I blame myself for not speaking to the Shah about this crass reaction to the response to his policy of liberalisation. It was not as though his loosening of the reins had evoked the forces of 'black reaction' or 'red revolution', his favourite bogeys. As I have said, the first manifestation of the new political freedom came from the moderate, centrist opposition, men and women whom he could have co-opted into a broader, more rational political structure than the aridities of Rastakhiz. Why then react first by ignoring them and then by thinly disguised state violence? Towards the end of the year, my staff pressed me hard to have this out with the Shah. They argued that I knew him as well as if not better than any other foreign Ambassador and that my careful avoidance of interference in Iranian internal affairs had given me a fund of credit with him on which I could well afford to draw at such an important moment. They were right. But I did not act. As bad luck would have it, our relations at the end of 1977 were in a peculiarly delicate state thanks to a corruption trial in London involving a serving British officer in which damaging allegations about the Shah were emerging in public. I was seeing Hoveyda, then Minister of Court, and the Shah frequently about the unfolding of this trial and was having a difficult time of it. The last thing I wanted was to add another bone of contention to my dialogue with the Shah. If Alam had been in office, I would have spoken to him; but he had gone. So I let the chance pass. It would almost certainly have made no difference if I had spoken, but the fact that I did not will always lie on my conscience.

Physical attacks on the moderate opposition were not by any means the only piece of dangerous buffoonery perpetrated by the regime in an atmosphere of rising ebullition. As I have mentioned before, the Shiraz International Festival had for many years been a subject of controversy because of the startling nature of some of the avant-garde performances staged in a traditional Muslim environment. Brazilian dancers biting the heads off live chickens and the presentation of the Shi'ite passion play, the Ta'ziye, as a stage performance for the entertainment of a mainly foreign audience are two examples which come to mind. The Shiraz Festival of 1977 excelled itself in its insults to Iranian moral values. For example, according to an eye-witness, a play was enacted which represented, as I was told, the evils of military rule and occupation. The theatre company had booked a shop in the main shopping street of Shiraz for the performance, which was played half inside the shop and half on the pavement outside. One scene, played on the pavement, involved a rape which was performed in full (no pretence) by a man (either naked or without any trousers, I forget which) on a woman who had had her dress ripped off her by her attacker. The denouement of the play, also acted on the pavement, included a scene where one of the characters dropped his trousers and inserted a stage pistol up his backside, presumably in order to add verisimilitude to his suicide. The effect of this bizarre and disgusting extravaganza on the good citizens of Shiraz, going about their evening shopping, can hardly be imagined. This grotesquerie aroused a storm of protest which reached the press and television. I remember mentioning it to the

Shah, adding that, if the same play had been put on, say, in the main street of Winchester (Shiraz is the Iranian equivalent of a cathedral city), the actors and sponsors would have found themselves in trouble. The Shah laughed indulgently.

The political effect of such an incident would have been bad enough at any time. It was especially so when there were many indications of an upsurge of religious traditionalism throughout the country. There had been religious inspired disturbances at Tehran University in October – possibly provoked in part by the Shiraz Festival – and threats had been made about the dress of female students; there was a strike against the practice of mixed cafeterias for the students. I recall that, in November, I visited Shiraz to read a paper at a seminar – a tailpiece to the British Cultural Festival – on Irano-British relations. The seminar was well attended by university students in spite of trouble on the campus, and all passed off peacefully. But I was intrigued, in the middle of reading my paper, by the arrival of about six girl students dressed in traditional black chadors with black head coverings. They sat silent and, it seemed, disapproving in the back row. On my way back to Tehran I was sitting in the aeroplane next to a friend of mine who had been attending the seminar, a Professor at Isfahan university. I mentioned the six black-clad girls and he told me that, during the past few months, there had been a remarkable increase of religious fervour at Isfahan university. He lived on the campus and it was not uncommon for him to find large student prayer meetings in progress in the open spaces after nightfall. How, I asked, did he explain this phenomenon? In his view, there had been a confluence between the radical Islamic student activists and the large number of new students, the beneficiaries of the Shah's education explosion, who were for the first time being drawn from small towns and even villages. These young people, coming as they did from a traditional and old-fashioned environment, found city life in Isfahan a shock, a translation to a modern Babylon. They therefore sought refuge in their religion and fell easy prey to the Islamic activists whose enthusiasms were heavily politicised.

I had further evidence of this disturbing trend from my friends in the universities of Tehran. I recall one particularly well informed professor at Aryamehr University (the technological university of Tehran) telling me that about 65 per cent of his students were motivated by Islam, about 20 per cent by communism, while the neutral remainder would always side with the Islamic group if it came to trouble.

Also in the autumn of 1977, Ayatollah Khomeini began to make his presence felt, albeit from his place of exile in Najaf, one of the two holy cities in the Shi'ite area of southern Iraq. One of Khomeini's sons had died – of course it was put about that he had been murdered by SAVAK – and many Iranians made pilgrimages to Najaf to offer their condolences to the old man. He took these opportunities to hold anti-regime seminars, the contents of which were recorded on cassettes and distributed in the bazaars of Tehran and elsewhere in Iran. This raised the religious temperature and it was significant that, in his implacable hatred of the Pahlavi dynasty, he never referred to 'Reza Shah' or the 'Shah'. The cassette recordings spoke of 'Reza Khan' and the 'son of Reza Khan', thus underlining his rejection of the legitimacy of the ruling monarchy.

The educated youth of Tehran were also finding different outlets to express their views in the new atmosphere of relative freedom, or at least of immunity from the mass arrests of the past. In October an important series of poetry-readings was held at the (West) German Cultural Centre at which Iranian poets read extracts from their works. One of these poets had been released from political detention only days earlier. He and others took the opportunity to voice powerful criticisms of the regime in the poems which they read. The audiences were huge, estimated at 62,000 over a period of a week, and demonstrably appreciative. There was no retaliation from the regime.

In late November, the Shah paid a state visit to Washington, the culmination of many diplomatic attempts throughout the year to develop a closer and less anxious relationship between him and President Carter. The students of Tehran and Aryamehr university made this the occasion to mount violent anti-Shah demonstrations and there were heavy clashes with the police on the campuses. At the same time, to the derision of the populace, Tehran television was showing film of the Shah and the Empress being ceremonially received by President and Mrs Carter at the White House. The considerable Iranian student body in the United States had been active and there were groups of anti-Shah demonstrators gathered outside the White House compound. The Iranian Ambassador in Washington had also been active and had recruited scores of loyalist counter-demonstrators. Clashes were inevitable between the opposing parties, and the police had to use tear gas. The wind carried the tear gas across the White House lawn and the Iranian television viewers were treated to the humiliating spectacle of their Shah and Empress, together with the President of the United States and Mrs Carter, standing stiffly at attention for the playing of the national anthems with handkerchiefs at their eyes and tears streaming down their faces. Had it not been for the era of liberalisation, I doubt whether these films would have been shown in Iran.

In November bad luck hit the Shah again. Earlier in the year he had lost to fatal illness his most powerful, wise and loyal adviser, Assadollah Alam. On November 25th, Dr Manouchehr Eghbal died suddenly of a heart attack. Dr Eghbal had never achieved the same intimacy with the Shah as Alam had, but he had known him for many years. He had served as Prime Minister and had latterly been the Chairman of the National Iranian Oil Company. After Alam, he was probably the only member of the inner circle who could have dared to try to influence the Shah: his age and distinction and his manner of an elder statesman gave him an entrée enjoyed by few. For months before his death, he, almost alone in the upper reaches of the government, had been speaking in private to his friends, including myself, in apocalyptic terms about the state of the country. This was a radical change from his self-confidence in previous years. On many occasions he impressed on me and, to my knowledge, on my best known predecessor, Sir Denis Wright (who was staying with me in Tehran), his acute concern at the direction the country was taking and his sense of impending disaster. I think that he expected us, the foreign friends of Iran, to transmit his apprehensions to the Shah. But I also believe that he was nerving himself to tackle the Shah direct shortly before his death.

I dined with him a week or two before he died and left his house with the impression that he was not prepared to remain silent much longer in the presence of his ruler. Had he spoken it might not have made any more difference than if I had spoken to the Shah about his failure to respond, except with violence, to the overtures which his people were making to him through their newly acquired freedom of expression. But, with the approaching storm, it was tragic that the Shah should have been deprived of the two men of distinction, Alam and Eghbal, who could have advised him well when his arrogance fell away and he was open to suggestions from those in whom he had confidence.

As the year closed, state violence, only thinly disguised, appeared to have done its work. The renascent moderate political elements, badly bruised by their experiences, were lying low again and the majority of university campuses were back at work. Officially, liberalisation was still the watchword and at least the policy of mass arrests had been put into abeyance. My assessment of the situation was sombre but not tragic. I feared that the wave of political activity might coalesce with the widespread social discontent, thus producing an inflammable concoction. The Shah was in a less confident mood, feeling his way carefully but clumsily regarding future political developments. He was still in control and I anticipated no threat to his regime. The problems he faced were troublesome rather than dangerous. In some ways the new spirit of realism, particularly in the management of the economy, seemed to me a sounder basis for progress than the arrogant over-confidence of the past.

Writing six years later, perhaps the saddest irony of 1977 was President and Mrs Carter's one-night visit to Tehran on New Year's Eve, December 31st. Accompanied by an entourage of about 500 officials, journalists and security men, the Presidential visit was intended to consummate the restoration of full confidence between the Shah and the American administration following the queasiness which had characterised Irano-American relations since January 1977. The great banquet at the Niavaran Palace was ostensibly private but the text of President Carter's after-dinner speech was widely circulated. I do not know who wrote his speech – my friends in the American Embassy loyally refused to tell me on New Year's Day – but its fulsomeness was breathtaking. I will gloss over the embarrassingly mawkish personal references and only mention that the President warmly lauded the Shah's Iran as an oasis of peace and stability in a troubled region and referred in glowing language to the love of the people of Iran for their Shah. Certainly the Shah could not have complained on that night of any trace of coolness in American support for himself and his dynasty.

SIX

1978-1979

For it is not always when things are going from bad to worse that revolutions break out. On the contrary, it oftener happens that, when a people which has put up with an oppressive rule over a long period without protest suddenly finds the government relaxing its pressure, it takes up arms against it. Thus the social order overthrown by a revolution is almost always better than the one immediately preceding it, and experience teaches us that, generally speaking, the most serious moment for a bad government is one when it seeks to mend its ways. Only consummate statecraft can enable a King to save his throne when after a long spell of oppressive rule he sets to improve the lot of his subjects. Patiently endured so long as it seemed beyond redress, a grievance comes to appear intolerable once the possibility of removing it crosses men's minds. For the mere fact that certain abuses have been remedied draws attention to the others and they now appear more galling; people may suffer less, but their sensibility is exacerbated.

De Tocqueville, *The Old Regime and the French Revolution*

January-September 1978

A few days after President Carter's departure, the government inadvertently lit the fuse that was to detonate the mine which, a year later, would destroy the Pahlavi dynasty and all it stood for. For some time the authorities had been getting worried about the inflammatory effect on public opinion of the clandestine Khomeini cassette recordings. In early January, someone decided that Khomeini must be openly discredited. Many people think that this was a personal decision by Daryoush Homayoun, the Minister of Information. But, in the fragmented structure of Pahlavi rule, it could have been a decision by the Shah, by SAVAK, or by the cabinet as a whole. No matter. It is enough to say that the method chosen was a piece of great foolishness which, even at the time, I believed would not have happened if Alam had still been at the Court or if Dr Eghbal had been alive. A long article was published in one of the leading newspapers traducing in lurid detail Khomeini's personal background, his private morals and his religious credentials. Coming as it did at a time of political and religious ferment unprecedented over the past fifteen years, the reaction was quick. On January 9th serious rioting broke out in the holy city of Qom, Khomeini's spiritual home. The situation passed beyond the control of the local police. Troops were called in, for the first time since 1963 and, whether through panic or by design, they fired into the crowd. A number of people were killed, fewer than ten according to the government, nearly a hundred according to the opposition. The whole country was shocked and staggered by the incident and a crisis developed between the Muslim religious leadership and the government. Several mosques in Tehran closed and the religious leaders announced that the customary forty-day mourning period would be observed for those killed at Qom.

After a few days, life appeared to return to normal and even the more perceptive members of the regime were full of confidence. I remember a revealing conversation I had with Hoveyda a few weeks later. I had been calling on him at his official residence near the Saadabad Palace compound in north Tehran one evening on routine business. We were chatting about some question which interested both of us when he said that he was late for an appointment with his dentist. As the latter's surgery was in south Tehran, farther away than my Embassy, Hoveyda offered to drive me down so that we could continue our conversation. We set off in his car with him driving and with no guard or escort. It was about 9 p.m. and the streets were well lit. When we got stuck in the first traffic jam, a number of pedestrians, as well as some workers in a lorry, recognised Hoveyda and crowded round the car. He opened the window and talked and joked with them. They kissed him and patted him on the back, a reassuring scene. When we moved on, I said that it was a pleasure to be driven by so popular a politician. He pointed out that he had been Prime Minister for thirteen years and had always gone out of his way to keep in direct touch with the people; I could see that he was not hated. The conversation turned to the internal situation and I expressed my anxiety at the way things were going. Why did the Shah not respond positively to the dialogue which his people were trying to conduct with him? What did he hope to gain by beating them into silence and by provoking a ghastly incident like the shooting at Qom? How bad was the situation in his view? I shall never forget Hoveyda's reply:

Well, Tony, you know His Majesty's definition of a dialogue. It is – I speak, you listen. He will not change. The government could do more. Amouzegar is brilliantly clever but he lacks a politician's touch with the people. I hope he will learn before it is too late that government is not entirely a matter of bureaucratic administration. The worst mistake he has made, in his passion to save government money, has been to cut off the large subsidy which I used to pay the mullahs, to keep them happy. I have been urging the Shah to restore it. However, things aren't all that bad. We only have to roll a few tanks down the main street of Tehran and it will calm down. We haven't had to do that yet.

I confess that I felt comforted by this conversation, more so when Hoveyda telephoned me a few days later to tell me, in guarded language, that the subsidy to the mullahs had been restored. The fact that he took the trouble to tell me this showed how much it had been on his mind.

But the lull did not last long. Exactly forty days after the incident at Qom, riots erupted in Tabriz, capital of Azerbaijan and the home base of Ayatollah Kazem Shariat-Madari, one of the leading Qom ayatollahs. This time the outbreak took the form of groups of people storming out of the mosques, burning and destroying property which was symbolic of Pahlavi modernisation, such as banks, liquor stores and the headquarters of Rastakhiz. Again the security forces were taken by surprise (the Chief of Police for Tabriz was subsequently sacked) and the garrison was called in. Even two tanks which were in the local ordnance depot for repair and teaching purposes were deployed in the streets (shades of Hoveyda's remark to me). More people died at the hands of the army and it was many hours before order was restored. The cycle of forty-day mourning periods was established.

I decided that I could no longer afford to maintain my self-denying ordinance about discussing internal affairs with the Shah. When I next saw him, I asked him point blank for his assessment of the situation in the light of the disturbances in Qom and Tabriz. I said that I knew he did not like discussing domestic affairs with foreign Ambassadors, particularly the British Ambassador, but I was not asking out of idle curiosity. We had a British community in Iran of about 20,000 souls; many of them were living and working in the provinces; there were upward of 500 British subjects in Tabriz. I therefore had a right to know how serious the situation was, for I had, apart from anything else, a responsibility for the safety and well-being of my compatriots.

The Shah was more realistic and less resentful at being drawn into conversation on such a ticklish subject than I had known him before. Yes, he said, the situation was serious but he was determined to press ahead with liberalisation. Many people, particularly SAVAK, were urging him to clamp down on dissidence but, as he saw it, there was no turning back. He had decided gradually to allow the people of Iran more freedom and he would not be deflected from this course. He did not particularly fear the communists and other radical elements drawn from the student body. The National Front and the other old political parties were not a serious threat. His most implacable enemies, and the most powerful, were the mullahs with their hold on the minds of the masses. There could be no compromise with them. They had never forgiven his father for not assuming the same relationship with the Shia' Church as that of preceding dynasties. Hence they had never recognised the legitimacy of his father as Shah, still less of himself. They could neither be bought nor could they be negotiated into co-operation with a regime which they did not recognise. It was a straightforward confrontation and one side had to lose. Although he did not say so in so many words, the Shah left me in no doubt that he could not imagine himself losing this battle.

Throughout the spring and early summer there was a spread of incidents on the Tabriz model in many cities, including Yazd in south-eastern Iran and in Tehran itself. In May the Tehran bazaar closed, a sinister portent: nothing like this had happened since the land reform riots of 1963. It became a commonplace for the army to be deployed against the rioters, and there were more fatal casualties, thus perpetuating the forty-day cycle of riots, deaths, forty days' mourning, further riots, further deaths, and so on. The government tried to organise counter-demonstrations through the Rastakhiz Party but these had little effect. One major effort of this kind in Tabriz, at which the Prime Minister and most of the Cabinet were present, was attended by a large and highly organised crowd - villagers were brought into Tabriz by bus from miles around - but there was little enthusiasm and, according to a friend of mine who was present, fights were constantly breaking out in the crowd between hired Rastakhiz supporters and opposition infiltrators. It was not an auspicious occasion.

And yet, it was surprising the extent to which normal life continued and how, in spite of the gravity of each individual incident, there appeared to be little or no evidence of a general build-up of tension. The Shah and the Empress came and went on state visits; they received the usual stream of visiting heads of state and other dignitaries. Foreign trade delegations poured into Iran and it was hard to imagine that we were living on the edge of a volcano. The Secretary of State for Defence, Mr Fred Mulley, visited Iran over the Now Ruz (Persian New Year) holiday in late March. He went down to the holiday resort of Kish Island on the Persian Gulf to see the Shah who received him cordially. The Shah looked fit and well and was very much in holiday mood. He had just returned from a morning ride with King Hussein of Jordan and the audience took place with dogs and children milling around the room. There was no sense of crisis. I remember that we stopped in Shiraz for a few hours on the way to Kish so that Mr and Mrs Mulley could do some sightseeing. We were told that there was trouble in the bazaar, but the atmosphere in the city was that of an English bank holiday with families happily picnicking on all available open spaces. Mr Mulley and I and our wives then flew to the Caspian for an informal luncheon with Hoveyda at his seaside bungalow. Nothing could have been pleasanter, more relaxed or informal.

Mrs Margaret Thatcher, then Leader of the Opposition, also visited Iran in April accompanied by the late Mr John Davies, then Shadow Foreign and Commonwealth Secretary. Her programme went without any hitches. The Shah received her, she called on leading ministers and addressed the Irano-British Chamber of Commerce at a large luncheon. The Prime Minister gave an interesting and entertaining dinner in her honour and she paid the normal sightseeing visits to Isfahan and Shiraz. Isfahan was full of European and American tourists, as was customary in the spring. The only evidence that everything was not entirely satisfactory was that Mrs Thatcher's visit to the Isfahan bazaar was quietly dropped, her escort explaining to me that there was 'the possibility of a little trouble there'.

This ostensibly full return to normality between incidents was outside my experience and lulled all of us into a false sense that the situation could not be so bad after all. I was accustomed to trouble in many Middle Eastern countries where, when a particular regime became unacceptably unpopular, there was usually a palpable and steady growth of tension, obvious even to the most superficial observer. But this was not the case in Iran in the first half of 1978. I remember visiting Yazd with my wife a few days after there had been a major clash there between rioters and the security forces, one feature of which had been the driving of dogs through the bazaar with placards reading 'Towards the Great Civilisation' attached to their hindquarters! We visited the textile factories and talked to the British technicians and managers working there. Yes, the riots had been serious and the factories had been on strike for a day or two. But, when we were there, everyone was back at work, the bazaars were open and my wife and I shopped and visited the principal mosques virtually unattended and with no sense of hostility or impending trouble. On another occasion at about the same period there had been a riot in the Tehran bazaar. The following day I had myself driven in my official Rolls-Royce, with the Union Jack flying, through the area immediately north of the bazaar. Again, no hostility, no sullen groups of people hanging around, no half-shuttered shops. Everything seemed calm and the populace were going about their business paying no attention to the conspicuous sight of the British Ambassador driving around an area where official diplomatic cars were seldom seen. It was as though each separate incident was a firework which flared up and died down again, leaving the surrounding area exactly as it had been before.

I was due to go on home leave for three and a half months towards the end of May, having not had a chance to escape from the pressures of Iran for over two years. I gave a great deal of thought to the situation in the country before taking this long break. I had sent a number of assessments to London. They ran broadly on the following lines. There was no doubt of the seriousness of the situation. The universities were in disarray and continuing student disorder, although not in itself a threat to the regime, was contributing significantly to public lack of confidence in the government's ability to solve its problems. The professional classes were up in arms at the Shah's dismal reaction to their demands for abandonment of censorship, an independent judiciary and political accountability of governmental agencies. Since the incident at Qom the religious classes had taken over the leadership of dissent and were openly inflaming passions through their sermons in the mosques. In spite of Amouzegar's efforts, the economy was wallowing. His deflationary policies were causing temporary hardship and the private sector was beginning to lose its nerve. The standstill budget for 1978-9 was on the right lines but its emphasis on essential infrastructure - education, low and medium cost housing, power generation and communications - would take a long time to produce beneficial results.

In a nutshell the Shah had lost the initiative and his liberalisation policy, which amounted to a tactic without an overall strategy, was merely whetting appetites for more. Rastakhiz was a fiasco and the Shah seemed content to let the chips fall where they might. If he failed to re-establish his position as national innovator, totally in control of events, the inconsistency of his claim to be the fountainhead of policy in a movement supposed to be inspired by the needs of the people might be exposed. The philosophy of the Shah–People Revolution contained no prescription for a time when the people became dissatisfied with the Shah's policies.

But I still did not believe that there was a serious risk of the Shah being overthrown. He had vast experience, the armed forces remained loyal, and he had lived through more difficult periods over the past thirty-seven years. He would continue his policy of liberalisation, confident that he could clamp down again without difficulty if need be. If it came to a clamp-down the armed forces would do their duty as they did in 1963 when the tribal khans and the religious leaders raised the standard of revolt against land reform. Furthermore the opposition was still disunited. Students, professionals, bazaaris and mullahs each had different sets of grievances and there was no sign of coalescence. It was not so much, as I saw it, that the regime was in danger, rather that the car had bogged down in soft ground and it was difficult to see how it could pick up speed again. I was still prepared to put my money on the Pahlavis, but I left for England in a far less confident state of mind than when I had last gone on home leave two and a half years previously.

When I returned to Tehran in early September, it was glaringly obvious that there had been a qualitative change for the worse and that the whole Pahlavi apparatus was in danger. In the meantime there had been a lull, in June and July, but serious disturbances had broken out in the fasting month of Ramadan (August 6th to September 4th). There had been a cycle of nightly violence with congregations, distempered by fasting and inflamed by the sermons of the mullahs, sallying from the mosques on the rampage against the symbols of modernity, Pahlavi-ism and non-Islamic culture. These outbreaks were sporadic, spontaneous, dispersed and difficult to control by the police and the military.

The religious leadership was far from united on objectives. Khomeini was demanding the overthrow of the Shah,

Shariat-Madari and the other ayatollahs of Qom and Mash-had were preaching the restoration of the 1906 constitution and the limitation of the Shah's powers; the Tehran mullahs were divided. But no one was prepared to call for calm and moderation for fear of being outflanked by the implacable and uncompromising Khomeini. The troubles got worse. On August 12th martial law was proclaimed in Isfahan and the Shah began to take palliative measures. He announced the total freeing of the press and speech and that new elections would take place in 1979. No one listened. The Shiraz Festival was, sensibly, cancelled. Then, on August 20th, there was a catastrophic fire in a cinema in Abadan in which 400 people died. The government blamed it on terrorists; the opposition accused the government of direct responsibility. The mass of the people believed the opposition. This was the straw which broke the Amouzegar government. On August 27th, Amouzegar, detested by the mullahs as an unsympathetic and anti-Islamic technocrat, resigned. The Shah replaced him with Senator Ja'afar Sharif-Emami, a man of impeccable religious credentials, the President of the Senate, but tainted by having been the head of the controversial Pahlavi Foundation. This amounted to an effort by the Shah to demonstrate a clean break with the technocratic past – whatever else he may have been, Sharif-Emami was no technocrat – and to show the people that he understood their wish to return to a more traditional, Islamic path.

It was a turning point, but not in the way the Shah intended. Sharif-Emami is believed to have made it a condition of his acceptance of the Prime Ministry that he should have a free hand and be seen to be genuinely in charge with the support of parliament; the Shah himself should take a back seat. The Shah's monopoly of power had been breached.

Sharif-Emami started by following the pattern of conciliation of the traditional forces which the Shah had begun a few weeks earlier. The Shah's beloved Pahlavi calendar, another preposterous affront to the religious suceptibilities of his people, was cancelled. (It had been inaugurated in 1976. The traditional Iranian year was solar as opposed to the Islamic lunar year, but in common with the Islamic calendar the dating began from the date of the Prophet Mohammed's flight (Hijra) from Mecca to Medina. However, on the fiftieth anniversary of the Pahlavi dynasty in 1976, the Shah decided that dating should begin from the accession of Cyrus the Great, about 1,000 years earlier. At the time this pointless piece of imperial arrogance excited the fury of the mullahs, the derision of the intelligentsia and the resentment of the masses.) All casinos were closed, also in deference to the religious temper of the main opposition movement; ironically Sharif-Emami, as Prime Minister, was closing the same casinos which, as head of the Pahlavi Foundation, he had only recently been instrumental in opening.

But these moves did nothing to check the rising tide. During the festival which marks the end of Ramadan, a vast but orderly demonstration, comprising all sections of society, marched from North to South Tehran. It was organised by the religious leadership with an efficiency which the state might well have envied. The demonstrators were hostile to the regime but peaceful. They fraternised with the troops and for the first time flowers were thrust into the barrels of the soldiers' rifles. There were no incidents but the generals were intensely alarmed by this massive demonstration of popular power and feared for the morale of the troops in the streets. The newly proclaimed freedom of the press – which, to the disbelief of any observer of only a few months previously, now began to print pictures of Khomeini on their front pages – added to the generals' alarm. The generals prevailed on the Shah and the Prime Minister to issue an edict banning further assemblies without prior authorisation.

Another huge demonstration took place, without permission, on September 7th, and a further one was planned for September 8th. The announcement that it would be forbidden was made late and many people have since argued that it would not have taken place if the organisers had known in time that the armed forces had been given orders to disperse the demonstrators. Others claim that many of the demonstrators of September 8th came armed with Molotov cocktails, their object being to provoke a clash with the military. Whatever the truth, a bloody confrontation took place between the

Imperial Guard and the demonstrators at Jaleh Square in south-east Tehran. The death toll will never be known for certain, but there is little doubt that hundreds fell to the automatic fire of the troops. Another turning point had been reached.

I had been in touch with the Foreign Office in London from late August; they in turn had consulted my Embassy in Tehran as to whether I should return prematurely to my post. The Embassy's advice was that I should not. The Shah and others knew that I was due back between September 10th and 15th and the Chargé d'Affaires, George Chalmers, rightly believed that my early return would do no good and would only exacerbate the sense of crisis in the minds of both government and opposition. I accepted this advice but kept in daily touch with the Foreign Office from the beginning of September. On the day of the affair at Jaleh Square, I was in the Middle East Department of the Foreign Office. I spoke on the telephone with the counsellor in the Embassy in Tehran, David Miers. I could hear the shooting in the background – Jaleh Square is only a mile or so from the Embassy compound – and again asked whether I should not return immediately. Chalmers and Miers stuck to their original advice. They assured me that there was no danger to British subjects and argued that I could do nothing useful by rushing back; in any case, after the bloody engagement there was likely to be a lull. I accepted their advice.

My wife and I flew back to Tehran on September 13th. When we drove the few miles through the city to the Embassy, I was immediately conscious of the atmosphere of generalised tension which had been so conspicuously absent even as late as the end of May. Tanks were deployed around the airport and there were scattered groups of soldiers in the almost empty streets; a night-time curfew was in force. There was now no doubt in my mind that a grim crisis was on us and that I had returned to a fundamentally altered situation. The validity of the Embassy advice to me not to advance my return was demonstrated the following day when I became aware of a rumour going round Tehran that the aircraft in which I had travelled – a scheduled British Airways flight – had somehow managed to land en route at Najaf in Iraq to enable me to consult with Ayatollah Khomeini on the progress of our joint effort to overthrow the Shah!

On September 16th I had my first private audience with the Shah after my return to Tehran two days earlier. I was horrified by the change in his appearance and manner. He looked shrunken: his face was yellow and he moved slowly. He seemed exhausted and drained of spirit. But he was ready to discuss the internal crisis without reserve or inhibition and gave me the unprecedented impression that he would welcome my personal view. He even asked at one point if we could influence the moderate mullahs into a more tractable frame of mind. I replied that, because of his suspicions of us, I and my immediate predecessors had avoided all contact with the religious classes. He must know that, and it was no use his expecting us now to do something which, if we had done it before, would have wrecked our efforts to build a good working relationship with him. The Shah smiled and accepted my point. He said that he was still determined to continue with liberalisation. He saw the present troubles, serious as they were, as part of a transitional period. The new government must prepare for genuinely free elections in June 1979. They had to build up their political strength. The opposition was well organised; the government was not. Rastakhiz had collapsed and the government had no alternative to offer. The anti-corruption drive had to be forced through and unpopular laws must be rescinded. Fortunately the armed forces had proved their loyalty and patriotism. He was confident in the regular soldiers but a little worried about the conscripts.

The Shah then asked plaintively why it was that the masses had turned against him after all that he had done for them. I replied that, in my view, there were many causes. The massive influx into the cities had produced a rootless and discontented proletariat. Many of them were engaged in construction work. They spent their days building houses for the rich and returned at night to shanties or even to holes in the ground lined with plastic. Crass materialism at all levels had led to insecurity when the good life had not arrived. It was no wonder in such circumstances that the people had turned to their traditional leaders, the mullahs who had always opposed the Shah. There was a yawning gulf of confidence between the government and the people. Iran had become a land of unfulfilled promises. I was having the same trouble with British firms. If I tried to interest them in a project, they were inclined to say that they had heard it all before – if they made the effort there would be a lot of talk and no action. The people of Iran felt the same way. As regards the opposition, I believed that Khomeini was implacable, and that nothing but the removal of the Shah would satisfy him. I was disposed to think the same of the National Front who could not have forgotten how the Shah had treated them after the fall of Mossadegh.

The Shah did not dissent from this analysis. At the end of our audience he asked me whether the British government still supported him. He hoped that we realised that any other regime in Iran would be worse from our point of view. I gave him the necessary assurance, pointing to a message which I had just delivered from the Prime Minister. He could take it from me that we were not hedging our bets, nor were we seeking reinsurance with any of the opposition elements. He seemed satisfied.

During the next two or three days I called on the new Prime Minister, Sharif-Emami, and on the new Foreign Minister, Amir Khosrow Afshar, an old friend from his days as Iranian Ambassador in London. I found both of them preoccupied with the impact of the BBC Persian language service broadcasts on the temper of the populace. This was an old chestnut and I was expecting it, having had a difficult time on the same topic at the beginning of 1978. On that occasion I had returned to London and had discussed the problem with those concerned at Bush House. It was, we all admitted, insoluble. The Iranian political establishment, from the Shah downwards, had never forgotten that the BBC Persian service had been created in the early days of the Second World War with the partial objective of de-stabilising the Shah's father's regime. It was impossible to convince anyone in Iran, even nearly forty years later, that Radio London, as it was called, was not the voice of the British government. I had done everything in my power to convince the Shah and his ministers that this was not the case; that the

BBC was independent; that it was not biased; and that what they regarded as subversive propaganda was actually nothing more than normal comment by an unfettered radio station. It was no use.

On this occasion, Sharif-Emami and Afshar, even the Shah himself, argued that, whatever the truth might be, 'the people' were convinced that the views of Radio London were the views of H.M.G. Some of the recent commentaries could only be interpreted as pro-Mossadegh and pro-National Front. Hence 'the people' had concluded that the British, the all-powerful British, had abandoned the Shah and were supporting the opposition. The mullahs themselves believed that they had British support which we were expressing through Radio London. Even Radio Moscow was being more circumspect than the BBC in its Persian language broadcasts. There was evidence that the BBC broadcasts were actually stimulating demonstrations and riots. I undertook to report these views to London but warned that, as in the past, there was nothing that we, as a government, could do except to relay their representations to the BBC. I suggested, as I had done many times in the past, indeed to Afshar himself when we had both been in London, that they would be best advised to instruct their extremely able Ambassador in London, Parviz Raji, to open a dialogue with the BBC based on accurate and factual evidence of offending broadcasts, rather than coming to me with unsubstantiated and second-hand accounts of BBC commentaries. It was his job, rather than mine, to try to influence the British media, including the BBC, regarding Iranian affairs.

This vexed question was to return to plague me throughout the coming months and I shall revert to it again. There is no doubt that my task of convincing my Iranian interlocutors of the independence of BBC foreign language broadcasts would have been easier were it not for the fact that these services are financed out of the budget of the Foreign and Commonwealth Office. It is hard to expect Third World autocrats, living in a tradition of state control of public information, to believe that, in this particular instance, he who pays the piper does not control the tune.

I saw the Shah again less than a week later. He looked fitter and was more alert. He was anxious to discuss the situation in detail – we talked for the best part of two hours – and to hear my views. He was worried that the Americans might be plotting with the opposition – he was of course expressing similar worries to my American colleague about British plotting – and wanted reassurance. I gave it. I emphasised that we were in the closest touch with the Americans in Tehran, London and Washington and that he could rest assured that there was complete unity of views between us. I went on to say that I even doubted whether the Soviet Union was actively supporting the movement to overthrow the regime. They would know that chaos would follow and my assessment was that they would prefer to have an orderly Iran under the Shah on their long southern border than an unpredictable Iran under whatever regime might replace him. My guess was therefore that, although they probably could not resist low-level meddling (for example by the provision of money to extreme left-wing groups), they were not active proponents of revolution in Iran. In my judgment, the troubles were caused by genuine and widespread internal discontent. The remedies were in the hands of the Shah and his government, not in searching for the hidden hands of foreigners. Emphasising, as I always did in these conversations, that I was speaking personally as someone who knew him well and not on instructions from London, I said that there must be free elections. The only alternatives were his overthrow or savage military repression. Also the government must try to produce quick and visible results in the economic and social fields. They must accommodate the moderate religious leadership. They must press on with liberalisation. I did not underestimate the dangers. Khomeini was determined to overthrow the monarchy and his following in the country was strong. There was little time available for the government to regain the confidence of the people. The Shah agreed. He said that he was no longer sure that his regime would survive. But liberalisation had to come; there must be a broad political base for his son to inherit, for the loyalty of the armed forces would not be enough. He had therefore given four main guidelines to Sharif-Emami's government. Firstly they must root out corruption. Secondly, they must open a dialogue with the moderate ayatollahs. Thirdly they must reallocate budget priorities away from expensive infrastructural projects towards immediate, visible benefits to the poor, particularly housing, schools and hospitals. Fourthly they must organise themselves politically so that they would emerge from the elections with a large block of pro-government deputies in the new parliament.

A few days after my return, I had called on Hoveyda. He was by that time out of office, living in his mother's tiny house in north Tehran. We sat in his study, a small comfortable room, the walls hidden by books. I asked him for his assessment of the crisis. He was anxious and apprehensive of the future, but by no means in despair. The main problem, as he saw it, was the Shah's inability to make up his mind and to show the people that he was directing a clear policy. If it was to be liberalisation and the full implementation of the 1906 constitution, so be it. If it was to be martial law and a return to harsh repression, so be it. But the Shah was vacillating. Martial law had been imposed, but was not being fully enforced. Sharif-Emami's palliative measures such as press freedom were being curtailed by the existence of martial law. Hoveyda said that the Shah was in desperate need of sound advice from disinterested people who had nothing but the country's best interests at heart. I asked whether he could fill this need. Hoveyda replied that it would be politically dangerous for him to appear at the palace, for if he were seen to be advising the Shah after his dismissal from the Ministry of Court, the Shah's reputation would suffer. He did however speak to the Empress from time to time on the telephone – 'She is the one with the guts.' As I left he urged me to keep in close touch with the Shah and to advise him wisely. I paid my respects to his mother and Hoveyda and I walked down the garden path together, past the numerous plain-clothes security guards with which he had been provided: 'I sometimes wonder whether they are here as warders or as protectors,' said Hoveyda as we parted.

In mid-September the tragic earthquake at Tabas in the Eastern Desert gave both the regime and the opposition an opportunity to bid for the allegiance of the people. The devastation caused by the earthquake, in which as many as

20,000 people died, was appalling – Tabas itself was virtually erased from the map.

The armed forces were responsible for relief operations but their efforts were vigorously supplemented by groups of mullahs, theological students and students from the university of Mashhad, all of whom worked hard to supply food and shelter to the survivors. After some delay, the Shah visited the area. Instead of going into the heart of the devastated town and sharing the grief and suffering of his people, he went no further than Tabas airport from which the military relief operations were being organised. Stiff and resplendent in a Field-Marshal's uniform, surrounded by bemedalled officers and security guards, the Shah looked ill at ease, and even Iranian television could not blur the contrast between, on, the one hand, the brief imperial visit and its isolation from the general suffering, and on the other the genuinely heroic efforts being made by the mullahs and students. A member of my family who was present as a freelance journalist confirmed to me that, from the point of view of the regime, the conduct of the relief operations and the imperial visit had been a public relations disaster.

Towards the end of September, I assessed the situation in the following terms. For the moment there had been a superficial return to something approximating to normality. The bazaars and schools were open and there was little overt evidence of the military in the streets of Tehran. Amazingly, the International Trade Fair was taking place attended by the normal crowds of peaceful Iranian families. The fiftieth anniversary celebrations of the foundation of the National Bank (Bank-e-Melli) were held on schedule, with the full Pahlavi pomp embracing the droves of foreign financial and economic dignitaries. But the underlying situation was very serious and Iran was unquestionably in the grip of the worst crisis it had experienced since the days of Mossadegh. The government must somehow get through the intervening months until elections could be held. Khomeini and the other extremists would do everything possible to prevent this. On the positive side the new Prime Minister was shrewd and resolute and had already started talking to the ayatollahs of Qom. He had for the moment taken the debate off the streets by emancipating discussion in the parliament and televising the proceedings – the population was riveted by this remarkable spectacle. On the darker side was the Shah's mood of depression and disillusionment. Hoveyda had put it to me that the Shah was suffering from a sense of total betrayal. He was like a man who had lavished everything for years on a beautiful woman only to find that she had been unfaithful to him all along.

I was still confident that the armed forces would do their duty and I thought that the Pahlavis had a fair chance of surviving, perhaps in a more acceptable and democratic form but with greatly reduced authority. But I could not for the life of me see how the government could solve the fundamental problem – to recapture the initiative from the burgeoning opposition without recourse to sterile and probably ineffective repression.

As regards our own policies, I held to the view that we should show no sign of wavering, reinsuring or hedging our bets. Our disproportionate influence was a two-edged sword. It was harmful when misleading impressions became current – the BBC and all that. It was advantageous in that the Shah and his government were prone to seek and to take our advice. If we were seen to be wavering in our support for the Shah, we would lose this asset and gain only the contempt of the opposition. The effect would be to compound the troubles of the regime.

October 1978

In the last days of September the illusion of normality evaporated, never to return. The mood of unrest revived. On September 29th and again on October 1st the Tehran bazaar closed in protest. Violent demonstrations became commonplace in the western and northern towns and cities which were not under martial law. And the strikes began, both in the public and private sectors. On October 1st workers and technicians in the National Iranian Oil Company, the Postal and Telegraph Administration, the Bank-e-Melli, the National Water Board, certain insurance companies and industrial enterprises went on full-scale or partial strike. Their demands were principally economic – higher pay, shorter hours of work, improved fringe benefits – and it was clear that the work force was taking advantage of the conciliatory policy of Sharif-Emami's government. But there were political undertones and Sharif-Emami told my American colleague and myself on October 3rd that the strikes were being fomented by a coalition of Khomeini, the Tudeh (Communist) Party and the National Front; whenever economic demands were met, political demands followed. I remember wondering at the time whether the Iranian people had hit upon the means of overthrowing the regime, even if the armed forces remained loyal to the Shah. I had been in the Embassy in Khartoum in 1964 when the Sudan was ruled by a military government under the Presidency of General Abboud. In the early autumn there had been a disturbance at Khartoum university and one or more students had been killed. Street riots followed but it did not look as though the government would have any difficulty in containing the situation. Suddenly the banned civilian political parties, including the communists, formed a National Front and called a national strike. The ministries, the airline, the railways, the state radio and many other institutions closed down; the strike committee allowed essential services to be provided – water, electricity, the telephone, food supplies – but nothing else. The army was helpless. They could clear the streets but they could not go from house to house and force everyone back to work. After a few days of this countrywide paralysis the military government admitted defeat and resigned. I speculated in my own mind and in many discussions with Sharif-Emami and the Shah during October whether the same thing might be on the point of happening in Iran: if the strikers gained their economic objectives and if the strike movement then turned political, this would be a far more sophisticated and effective method of embarrassing the government than rioting, and far more difficult for the military to counter.

Meanwhile Khomeini moved to Paris in bizarre circumstances. Sharif-Emami sent for my American colleague and myself on two occasions in early October. He first told us that Khomeini was on the move and that the Iraqi government would be glad to see the back of him. It seemed that the old gentleman was actually in a car, probably heading for Kuwait. Sharif-Emami's worry was that he would slip across the head of the Persian Gulf in a boat and suddenly appear in Iran. Sharif-Emami believed that, if this happened and Khomeini was allowed to go free, the regime would be swept away. If he were arrested on crossing the frontier, there would be civil war. However, if the worst came to the worst, he would have Khomeini arrested and risk the consequences. Could we, the British and Americans, persuade the Kuwaiti government not to allow Khomeini to cross the Kuwaiti frontier? I said that I was reluctant to recommend such action to my government although I would of course report the conversation. Khomeini was Iranian – I discovered from Sharif-Emami that his passport had been recently renewed by the Iranian Consulate in Baghdad – and Iran had a perfectly good Ambassador in Kuwait. There was also a senior and responsible Kuwaiti Ambassador in Tehran. Sharif-Emami should approach the Kuwaitis direct, not through us.

At our second meeting on this subject on October 4th, Sharif-Emami told us that the Iraqis had made an unsuccessful attempt to persuade Khomeini to keep out of politics. They now had no intention of preventing him from leaving Iraq. Khomeini was still roaming around in southern Iraq; he had been refused entry to Kuwait and Sharif-Emami thought that he might fly to Syria or possibly to Algeria. In the meantime there was still a danger that he might make a dash for the Iranian frontier by road or, even worse, arrive unexpectedly by air at Tehran airport. In either case he would be arrested.

On October 7th the news broke that Khomeini had flown to Paris where he was joined by his three devoted followers, Abol Hassan Bani Sadr, Sadegh Ghotbzadeh, and Ibrahim Yazdi (the first now back in exile in Paris, the second executed for allegedly plotting against Khomeini, the third in disgrace). I was calling on the new Minister of Court, Ardalan, shortly after Khomeini's flight. My French colleague was with the minister and I had a long talk to his Vice-Minister, Homayoun Bahadoori, a close friend. We were both inclined to think, as were the Shah and Sharif-Emami, that Khomeini had made a mistake in leaving the Muslim world for a Christian capital. His religious influence and hence his political power might decline. (We were of course hopelessly wrong: as all the world knows, Paris provided Khomeini with a matchless public platform from which to conduct his campaign to destroy the Shah. But, at the time, many intelligent and well informed Iranians shared the view that Khomeini had slipped up.) I remember Bahadoori asking me what I thought the French government would do and what we would do if Khomeini decided to move to London. I said that both France and Britain had a long tradition of receiving political exiles. In our case we had a visa abolition agreement with Iran and, since the Iranian authorities had been obliging enough to re-validate Khomeini's passport, there would be nothing we could do to stop him entering the United Kingdom. If he did, he would be free to go where he liked and to say what he liked provided that he did not infringe British (not Iranian) law. I assumed that the French position would be roughly the same. I admitted to Bahadoori that I was keeping my fingers crossed that the Ayatollah's known dislike of Britain would spare us the embarrassment of his presence, although the Iranian government must realise that we would not infringe our own laws on their behalf either by refusing him admittance or by muzzling or deporting him, provided that he did not misbehave.

By this time riots and demonstrations were again swirling in the streets of Tehran. On October 7th the new university term had started, to my mind a mistake. I had expressed the strictly personal view either to the Shah or to Sharif-Emami – I think the latter – that if the university students assembled in their campuses, they would obviously refuse to attend classes. Their ingathering would enable them to muster and mobilise to challenge the authorities on the streets, whereas they would be unable to do so if the bulk of the students remained scattered in their home towns throughout Iran. So it turned out. Within a few days of their reassembling, the university students of Tehran had abandoned their customary campus demonstrations in favour of marches and processions in the main streets of the capital. Large bands of schoolchildren, male and female, who were also refusing to attend classes, followed suit. There were more sinister groups abroad, roughly dressed, youngish middle-aged men, armed with iron bars and wooden clubs. Many people thought these thugs to be SAVAK agents provocateurs or Imperial Guardsmen in civilian clothes. Who knows? All I remember is that Bill Sullivan, my American colleague, and I had a slightly over-stimulating experience with one such group on our way back from one of our meetings with Sharif-Emami. Sullivan was travelling with me in my Rolls-Royce with his car following behind. When we reached a point only a few hundred yards from my Embassy, we realised that the usual traffic jam had been compounded by the approach of a demonstration comprising about a hundred disagreeable-looking men. I suggested to Sullivan, who agreed, that we should remain on course in the Rolls and see what the reaction was when the demonstrators came abreast of us. When they were about fifty yards away, we saw that they were overturning and wrecking all the cars in their path. Sullivan's eyes met mine. 'Let's go,' we said simultaneously, discretion quickly overcoming valour. My driver, with great skill, managed to turn in the crowded street and we shot off down a small alley pursued by some of the club wielders. My driver, again with considerable presence of mind, drove into the car-park of a nearby bank which Sullivan and I, followed by our plainclothes police escorts, entered. The police and bank officials locked the doors, somewhat to the distress of the many people who were going about their normal business in the bank, and we were taken to the manager's office. He received us with great charm and sang-froid, gave us tea, and we discussed the economic and financial situation of Iran for an hour or so. When the streets had cleared, Sullivan and I walked back to our respective Embassies; it had been a longer morning than we had anticipated.

By mid-October the situation appeared desperate but not entirely hopeless. Sharif-Emami was still talking to the Qom ayatollahs, although he told me that they could not compete with the large sums of money which Khomeini was channelling to the theological students and bazaar proletariat to keep up the pressure on the regime through intimidation of waverers. The Prime Minister was also dramatising the anti-corruption drive. The former Minister of Health, Shaikholeslamzadeh, and two of his deputies were arrested because of complicity in an alleged hospital construction project involving the family of the Empress. The former Ministers of Agriculture and Commerce, Rouhani and Mahdavi, were arrested. The head of the Atomic Energy Department, Etemad, was dismissed. Eighteen businessmen and administrators were detained. Fifteen separate investigation teams were established and the Shah issued an instruction that the Imperial Family was not to indulge in any commercial activity: an investigation into all the Pahlavi endowments was launched. The then Governor of the Bank-e-Melli, and General Nassiri, former head of SAVAK (replaced in June by General Nasser Moghaddam) and then Ambassador to Pakistan, fell under suspicion. Nassiri was recalled to be examined by a military tribunal. All this activity was in principle salutary but it came at a time when it further threatened the fabric of the state, particularly since junior officials of the investigation teams made a point of revealing lurid details about all and sundry to the press, domestic and foreign, as they pursued their investigations.

The government continued the policy of liberalisation. More political prisoners were released and laws were passed establishing academic freedom, rights of the press and the freedom of assembly. Again these measures were the right ones but they attracted little attention in comparison to Khomeini's simple message that the Shah must go. It was more than ever clear that the key lay not with the National Front politicians, who were making little headway, not with the students nor the extremist groups of right and left, not even with the government. The future would depend on the attitude of the religious leaders. Would Khomeini's fundamentalist, anti-Pahlavi doctrine sweep everything away or was there a chance that the more moderate ayatollahs of Qom and Mashhad would prevail with their less radical demand for a strict application of the terms of the 1906 constitution, including a reduced role for the Shah? In brief the focus of political activity had moved outside the recognised institutions of Shah, government and parliament.

I assessed the situation of the government many times in

the first half of the month. I concluded that there had been a fundamental and irredeemable shift of power. Iran was now tripartite regime. The Shah was sitting in the background at the Niavaran Palace, intriguing with various political personalities without prior co-ordination with the Prime Minister. The latter was trying to run the country and at the same time take measures to defuse the crisis – holding talks with the religious leaders, pursuing the anti-corruption drive, rescinding unpopular legislation and so on. Thirdly the military were uneasily holding the ring, with the generals becoming increasingly restive at Sharif-Emami's conciliatory policies. The military machine was still more or less intact but we were starting to ask ourselves, with growing frequency, how long they could hold out in the face of continuing disorders and, more important, the paralysing weapon of the strike.

Although there was a slight lull around mid-October and the situation looked fractionally better, with moderate opposition politicians apprehensive about the forces which had been unleashed and with the newly emancipated press calling for responsible behaviour at a time of national crisis, there was no question in our minds but that the underlying situation was bleak in the extreme. For a time the strikes widened to include government hospitals, the national airline (Iranair), school teachers, junior staff in ministries, and the government media. A bandwagon of civil disobedience was on the move and, although Sharif-Emami from time to time appeared to be getting control of the strike situation, there always seemed to be a recrudescence, each time more deeply coloured by political demands. Meanwhile the generals were pressing the Shah to allow them to clamp down on the growing disorders which they attributed to Sharif-Emami's liberal policies. The freeing of the press was a particular bone of contention and there were occasions when, on the orders of the generals, newspaper offices were invaded and journalists arrested. Strikes followed and were only settled when the Prime Minister re-established his authority over the military. On October 17th the government formally proclaimed the end of censorship and guaranteed freedom for the press. Resentment amongst the military was exacerbated by this move and the civil and military arms of government became in effect adversaries. In mid-October, Sullivan and I called on General Oveissi, the Martial Law Commander, with the approval and support of the Prime Minister. We told him that rumours were circulating in the officer corps that Britain and America would favour a military takeover of the government. We wanted him to know that these rumours were baseless. Both our governments favoured progressive democratisation as the only way to solve the crisis. A reversal of this process would face us with severe problems of domestic opinion in our own countries. The effect of a military coup on Iran's Western friends and allies would be disastrous. Other rumours of diminution of British and American support for the Shah were untrue. General Oveissi took our points without enthusiasm.

Another negative factor in the equation was the public effect of the Shah's loss of morale. He made two good speeches on Iran television during October, one about liberalisation and the other about the legitimacy of the monarchy. What he said was cogent and well thought out, but his listless and dispirited manner created a poor impression. Respect for and awe of him evaporated and I concluded towards the middle of the month that the best that could possibly be expected was that he might, if everything went well, recover enough prestige to act as a purely constitutional monarch – no more.

In the second half of October there was a pronounced all-round deterioration and it was evident that Sharif-Emami's government was doomed. They could do nothing to solve the problem of turbulence in the schools and universities and the streets were daily filled with student demonstrations leading to bloody clashes with the troops. Because of the persistent strikes the government was in no position to stimulate the economy and the rift between Sharif-Emami and the military commanders was becoming daily more dangerous. Sharif-Emami still believed that strong nerves and stamina could win the day and that it was a question of who would run out of steam first. But the extreme opposition was thrashing along at a furious rate and there was no sign of their impetus slowing down. The waves of crisis followed each other so quickly that it became impossible accurately to foresee the future. The strikes in the oilfields spread and seriously damaged production. The demands of the strikers became overtly political – the return of Khomeini and the lifting of martial law. Houshang Ansari, Chairman of NIOC, went to the south to negotiate but was mobbed by the strikers and, after a few days, left for Paris; he never came back. There was a recrudescence of violent disturbances in the provinces and the first signs of an incipient anti-foreign groundswell, particularly in the oilfields.

Against this sombre background the Shah decided that he must act. He remained implacably opposed to a military takeover – 'A military solution is no solution' – but he realised that it was no longer a question of trying to survive until free elections could take place in June 1979. That date, which had seemed so close only a month or so previously, now appeared to be a world away. The crisis was on him and the outcome must come soon. On October 31st he told me that something had to be done quickly – 'We are melting away daily like snow in water.' He said that the situation must be brought under control before the holy month of Moharram (December). Sharif-Emami could not regain the initiative. He was a brave man and had done his best. But the oilfields were paralysed, the demonstrations and riots uncontrollable, the strikes were killing the country and the students were out of hand. If the crisis was not solved before Moharram he would be faced with the choice of surrender – his own departure – or a complete clamp-down which would be bloody and would ultimately solve nothing. He had decided against a military government and was looking for a government which could calm the country and resume the forward movement to democracy. The only answer was to find a neutral and prestigious figure who was untainted by association with the regime over the past fifteen years. This person would lead a caretaker government including the National Front and the Pan-Iranist Party and excluding all members of the present government. Its terms of reference would be to prepare for immediate elections, and to prosecute the anti-corruption drive. His nominee for the post of Prime Minister was Abdollah Entezam, the respected former Foreign Minister. Admittedly he was over eighty years old but he fulfilled the necessary conditions. Failing him he would ask Sururi, former Head of the Supreme Court. He was even older but a man of blameless reputation. If he would not accept, then he would ask Ali Amini, formerly Finance Minister in the 1950s and Prime Minister in the early 1960s.

The Shah had been working up to this decision for some days and, as he became more actively involved in the crisis, his morale improved. He was prepared to examine every feature of the abyss which yawned before him with admirable composure and objectivity. He was equally determined not to try to buy a respite by bloody military action. Even his sense of humour had not deserted him. When I queried Entezam and Sururi on grounds of age and infirmity he replied that Entezam was rather deaf but he thought he would accept the post if he could hear what it was that was being offered him. And Sururi was 'probably still strong enough to walk the few yards to the parliament building for his confirmation'.

Sullivan and I agreed with the Shah's assessment. We had throughout supported Sharif-Emami in our conversations with the Shah and had opposed military intervention – I had on many occasions told the Shah of my experience in the Sudan and warned him of the risk that, if he appointed a military Prime Minister, there would be a national strike which only his own departure from Iran would break. He never dissented from this judgment. Both Sullivan and I urged the Shah to accelerate the electoral process as much as possible in order to focus people's minds on something more constructive than rioting, demonstrating and striking. We also warned him against allowing a witch-hunt to take place against members of former cabinets and other prominent personalities of recent years. On this point the Shah was equivocal and I feared that he was contemplating a policy of throwing people to the wolves in order to enable him to draw clear of the pursuit. Nassiri would have to go to jail, he said, probably Hoveyda as well – two of his most devoted and longest serving adherents dismissed in a sentence.

Meanwhile Khomeini was pouring out invective against the regime and issuing instructions to the people of Iran to oppose the government, to engage in civil disobedience and

86

to withdraw all forms of co-operation from the monarchy – all from his villa near Paris. His fulminations were disseminated in Iran by many means – through the distribution of cassette recordings, through publication in the newly freed press, via the Persian language service of the BBC. By settling in a sophisticated Western capital with all the resources of modern communications at his disposal and media representatives from all over the world beating a path to his door, he had an unrivalled rostrum, far more effective than if he had remained in Iraq or moved to another Muslim country such as Syria or Algeria. Those of us, including myself, who had thought that he might have made a mistake in leaving the Islamic world for a Christian capital had been proved comprehensively wrong. Throughout October, as his simple message waxed louder and more insistent, it drowned the voices of moderation. Sharif-Emami tried unsuccessfully to reason with him. In the first half of the month he sent emissaries to Paris to make three points to Khomeini. Firstly, his agitation had already lost hundreds of Muslim lives. Was this proper conduct for an ayatollah? Secondly, he would not bring the Shah down. The latter would still be on the throne when Khomeini was dead. Thirdly, if he returned to Iran he would be arrested. No response. By the end of October Khomeini's star was strongly in the ascendant and National Front leaders, headed by Karim Sanjabi, as well as emissaries from Ayatollah Kazem Shariat-Madari and Mehdi Bazargan were in Paris trying to negotiate a united opposition programme with Khomeini's endorsement. This was not an auspicious setting for the Shah's attempt to create a coalition government to include the leadership of the National Front but, right until the end of the month, he had been pinning his faith on Sharif-Emami and had been reluctant to co-opt the Front for fear of the extreme demands they would make as conditions for co-operating.

Before I go on to describe the crucial events of early November which finally extinguished any faint hope that might previously have existed for the Shah's survival, it might be useful if I recapitulated the advice I had been giving him through October, sometimes in the company of my American colleague, sometimes alone. I emphasise again, as I did on every occasion to the Shah, that I was not advising him on instructions from London, although the FCO would have been quick to tell me if they had thought that my advice was ill judged. At the beginning of each of our long, repetitious, and circular examinations of the crisis, I would stress to the Shah that I would only give my opinions if asked and that they were my personal views, not the product of some sinister plot hatched in London. At the time he accepted these assurances, as indeed he was right to do.

The burden of my analysis in my discussions with him was that the ferocious outburst of public emotion was a natural consequence of the fifteen years of severe repression which he had imposed on Iran while he pressed on with his modernisation programme. Since modernisation had ridden roughshod over the traditional forces of Iran and had produced gross inequalities of wealth and appalling conditions for the urban poor, it was no wonder that the wave of emotion had become a wave of opposition. The fact that he was the target was also natural. For years he had presented himself as the sole, inspired leader and had reduced his ministers and the parliament to cyphers. He had taken all the credit in the good times and it was inevitable that he should take all the blame in the bad times; he was now suffering the consequences of deliberately eliminating all buffers between himself and the people. The Shah-People Revolution was recoiling on his head.

All of us had anticipated that, when he liberalised, there would be a redistribution of power between him, the government and the parliament. The transitional period was bound to be dangerous and, as it turned out, the clergy's innate opposition to him, plus Khomeini's prestige and glamour, had canalised the wave of opposition into an extremist torrent which would not stop short of the overthrow of the regime. Nobody could have anticipated that events would move so fast and it was no longer serious to think in terms of elections in the summer of 1979 – they could not take place too soon.

Until the last days of October I counselled the Shah to support and retain Sharif-Emami. It seemed to me that he was showing nerve, stamina and courage and that he was steadfastly pursuing the only path which might outlast the opposition and calm the country, namely to keep ahead of the extremists by accelerating the process of democratisation and liberalisation. Any change of government in my view would be interpreted as a sign of weakness and stimulate the opposition to redouble their efforts. And, in spite of the strikes, the student unrest and the violence, the government still had the tools of power while the opposition had only emotional agitation on their side. Until it was clear at the end of the month that Sharif-Emami had shot his bolt, I advised the Shah against trying to co-opt the National Front into the government. My feeling was that, because of their treatment at his hands in the immediate post-Mossadegh era, they were probably as implacably opposed to him as Khomeini and would only co-operate on terms which would amount in effect to the end of the monarchy.

As the fury of the storm grew after the brief lull in mid-October, I modified my opinion about the desirability of bringing the National Front into the government. By the time the Shah had come to his decision that a coalition government including the National Front was the best expedient, it was clear that civil authority under Sharif-Emami had disintegrated and that a radical reconstruction of the government was necessary. But I continued to advise against the appointment of a military government. As I have suggested, I had two principal reasons for this. First, the military were totally inexperienced in governing a complex state such as Iran and I did not believe that they would get the minimal co-operation necessary from the civil bureaucracy to carry out their tasks. Second, and more important, I was convinced that the advent of a military government would immediately provoke a nationwide strike which would paralyse the country and lead to the early collapse of the regime. I advanced these views on many occasions to the Shah during October, drawing on the Sudanese parallel, and, so far as I could judge, he never disagreed, although my views earned me the resentment and hostility of the military commanders.

November 1978

On November 1st, Sullivan and I had another audience with the Shah. By this time riots in the provinces were a daily occurrence, although there were a few pro-Shah counter-demonstrations; the strikes were continuing and the streets of Tehran were choked with student marchers. It was difficult to travel from south Tehran, where my Embassy was situated, to the Niavaran Palace on the northern outskirts. I was twenty minutes late for my audience with the Shah, having made a series of detours to avoid the demonstrations on the lateral streets. Sullivan was there when I arrived. The Shah told us that he had persuaded Entezam to lead a new government. He had also received a message from Karim Sanjabi in Paris that he had persuaded Khomeini to call off his attacks on the regime on condition that an immediate referendum was held on the monarchy. The Shah had heard that the National Front were moderating their position in the light of the seriousness of the situation. He did not intend to reply directly to Sanjabi's message but would invite the National Front leaders to meet him to discuss joining a coalition government under Entezam. The Shah was in a sombre mood. He believed that it was now a matter of days rather than weeks. Pressure from the generals was growing. They were urging him to allow them to take over and 'save the country'. He was arguing that this would solve nothing. Even if he failed to form a coalition government with the National Front, he would still not call in the military. He would adopt what he considered to be the last resort, the formation of a neutral government of elder statesmen solely to carry out free elections as quickly as possible. I warmly endorsed his strategy.

On November 4th Sullivan and I were again summoned to the palace, this time for what turned out to be one of the most dramatic of our many meetings with the Shah. Sullivan told me in the ante-room that he had received some instructions from Washington. The Shah opened by telling us that he had received a telephone call from Zbigniew Brzezinski, head of the National Security Council in Washington. Brzezinski had told him that the US government would support him either for the formation of a coalition government or a military government. The Shah asked us for the reactions of our respective governments if he appointed a military Prime Minister. Sullivan made clear that Brzezinski's telephone call did not mean that the United States favoured the military option, rather that they would go along with it if the Shah decided that he had absolutely no other choice. I said that I had no specific instructions from London. However, as the Shah knew, my government was firmly in favour of a political solution. Speaking personally, I reminded him that I myself had suggested the alternative of a neutral, caretaker government if the coalition idea failed. He knew my views on what could happen if he brought in the military and I still held to them. Nevertheless, he was a sovereign ruler and I felt confident that my government 'would respect' whatever decision he finally felt that he had to take.

The discussion, which lasted about two hours, then became more diffuse. The Shah said that he was still trying for a coalition and that the National Front leaders were due to see him the following day. He would have nothing to do with Sanjabi's proposal of a national referendum on the monarchy. Meanwhile the generals were pressing him harder than ever, their view being that they could calm things down easily by making a number of arrests (at this point I sensed that the generals knew of the Brzezinski telephone call and that this might account for their heightened pressure on the Shah). The Shah went on to say that it was all very well for Brzezinski to talk, but he still believed that unleashing the military would solve nothing. For the last time, I restated my view that military intervention would be followed by a national strike with which the army would be unable to cope: they could clear the streets but they could not force people out of their homes and back to work. The situation was quite different from the Mossadegh crisis in 1953 to which the generals kept harking back. Then, Mossadegh did not have the support of the mullahs, and the people as a whole were neutral. The only violent activity had been in Tehran and in the oilfields. There had been no student problem. Today the dimensions of the crisis were vastly greater and the forces deployed against the regime more universal and more formidable. I had seen many military takeovers in my career. They had been successful in the short term because the people as a whole had welcomed or at least acquiesced in them. This would not be the case in Iran.

I returned to my Embassy late in the evening with considerable foreboding. It had been a bad day in the city and elsewhere in the country. Large and violent demonstrations had taken place in many areas of Tehran; cars had been burnt and there had been more civilian casualties at the hands of the army. Tension had reached breaking point. My talk with the Shah had done nothing to allay my fears. I sensed that the coalition idea was foundering and that the Shah would not be able to resist his generals much longer, particularly if my assumption was correct that they believed the US government would support a military takeover. I could see little or no hope for the future.

The following day, November 5th, the balloon went up. I was working in my office at about 10 a.m. when I was told that an emissary from certain religious leaders wanted to talk to me immediately. I decided to see him. He told me that he had just returned from Paris where he had seen Khomeini and the National Front and other politicians who had been there at the same time. He could confirm to me that Sanjabi, and hence the National Front as a whole, would not join the coalition because of Khomeini's opposition. He, my visitor, would be going to Qom in a few days' time to report to the religious leaders there. Their view was that the only way to save Iran from complete disaster was for the Shah to leave the country and temporarily to cede power to a Council of State to be headed by a distinguished, retired military officer. The Council would appoint a government of national reconciliation which would hold elections as soon as possible. When the newly elected parliament met, its first task would be to take a vote on whether Iran should be a monarchy or a republic. He and the religious leadership in Qom were confident that such a vote would go in favour of the monarchy, provided that the 1906 constitution was strictly adhered to. He knew that I saw the Shah frequently and asked me if I would put this proposition to him.

In reply I first urged him to return immediately to Qom

for consultations with his masters there. There was no time to lose – he must have noticed on his way to my Embassy that people were gathering in unprecedented numbers for a demonstration to celebrate the release from political detention of Ayatollah Taleghani (a leading Tehran mullah who had been in prison for some years). It looked to me as though everyone on the side of moderation might have run out of time.

As regards his proposal, I said that, if the Shah asked me for the views of the opposition, I would tell him what had been said to me. But I was a foreign Ambassador, not a player in the Iranian political game. I would not act as an intermediary between the Shah and the opposition: it would be both improper and ineffective. Why did he not go himself to the palace and put forward his ideas? He laughed. 'Because I know that, if I enter the Niavaran, I will never come out.'

After he left, I decided that I should share my knowledge with Sullivan. I set off in my Rolls-Royce (almost the last time I ever used it) for the drive of about half a mile to the American Embassy. It was by now about 11.30 a.m. and the pavements were crowded with people, trudging along to join the great demonstration. They were peaceful, silent, intent and took no notice of my conspicuous presence. But the feeling of extreme tension was palpable.

After Sullivan and I had finished our discussion and I was preparing to return to my Embassy, I was told that this would be impossible for some hours, for the demonstration was under way and all streets between our two Embassies were completely blocked by people. Sullivan kindly asked me to stay to lunch and to return when the streets had cleared. I was of course in touch with my staff by telephone and confirmed that all was quiet at their end. At about 2 p.m. Sullivan and I heard explosions and saw columns of smoke rising from buildings to the north of the American Embassy. We made enquiries and it emerged that, in the centre of the city, small groups of people, mainly young men, were on the rampage, burning and destroying buildings which had any connection with the hated regime and its policies – banks (money was being piled in the streets and burnt, not looted), insurance companies, the office buildings of major state and private enterprises, shops selling liquor, etc. As this wave of destruction showed no sign of abating and as the peaceful demonstration had by this time dispersed, I decided to return to my Embassy, having learnt on the telephone from my secretary that there was no activity of any kind near our building. I set off cautiously in a Peykan car which Sullivan lent me, leaving my Rolls-Royce in his compound, with a second escort car full of plain-clothes policemen. When we emerged into the main street, I found myself faced by a scene such as I had not experienced since the end of the Second World War. Fires were burning everywhere, furniture and office equipment had been piled in the middle of the street and set alight, burning cars and buses littered the roadway. Young men were dancing around in a frenzy, feeding the flames and plastering the few passing cars with stickers reading 'Death to the Shah'. We edged forward slowly, our own car bedecked with stickers and with excited demonstrators riding on the roof. As we rounded Ferdowsi Square, a few hundred yards from my Embassy, the road was almost entirely blocked by blazing cars and buses. My driver negotiated these obstacles with difficulty, but I saw that the police escort ahead was in trouble. The rioters had seen the police radio inside the car; they had wrenched open the doors and were trying to drag the occupants out. The last I saw of my escort, who eventually found their way back to the American Embassy, was the car careering down a side street with three of its doors open and a mob of young men clinging to the sides. We drove on, with our burden of students on the roof, responding appropriately to menacing shouts of 'Death to the Shah' which were being bellowed through the car windows; for the moment I had joined the revolution. When we came abreast of the Embassy, I saw that a few people were throwing stones at the windows from across the street and a small crowd was gathering outside the gate. My driver drove up to the gate and we all got out. The gate was (rightly) locked and I could not attract the attention of anyone inside the compound – it looked deserted. We backed out and drove on, intending to enter by the rear door to the Consulate which was at the other side of the walled compound. As the car rounded the corner I saw a platoon of infantry with an armoured car. They were standing there taking absolutely no notice of what was going on. The rear door too was locked. I decided to go on to the French Embassy, about half a mile away, from which I could get in touch with my staff and gain access to the compound through the rear door. My French colleague could not have been more helpful but, by the time I got through on the telephone, a crowd had stormed my Embassy and I was stranded. I decided that the best thing I could do was to use the French Embassy telephone to contact the military command, the Prime Minister and others to try to ensure that my Embassy was given belated protection and the crowd driven off. I had great difficulty in getting in touch with anyone in authority. Eventually I spoke to General Azhari, Chief of Staff to the Commander-in-Chief. I asked him formally and with some asperity to clear out any rioters who might still be in the British Embassy compound and to guarantee us adequate protection. I ended up by asking him what he was doing to bring the overall situation in the city under control. 'It is all your fault,' he replied, 'you have been persuading His Majesty for too long to stop us from intervening and restoring the situation.' But he promised to take the necessary steps to protect the Embassy. By nightfall the streets had more or less emptied and the army, which had remained passive observers of the destruction and burning throughout the day, had imposed a curfew. I returned to my Embassy under military escort past the gutted buildings and the still burning cars in the streets, to find yet another scene of chaos. A smallish group had scaled the fence in front of the Chancery building and had set fire to part of the offices, assisted by a consignment of bottled gas which had been delivered to the Embassy that day. The guardhouse at the gate had been destroyed and a large part of the office building damaged by the fire. The far end of the building which housed our non-confidential commercial archives (testament to the boom years) had been gutted. One of the domestic houses, occupied by a British security officer and his family, had been broken into and damaged. The rioters had made no attempt to hurt any of the staff or their families and all the other domestic buildings, including my Residence, were unharmed. The strongroom

containing all the confidential documents was intact. Needless to say the power and telephone lines had been burnt
through and we spent the night incommunicado and in pitch
darkness. I found my staff and their families, including my
wife, slightly shaken but in excellent heart. It is unnecessary
to add that everyone had behaved admirably and that all
concerned were immediately determined to restore the Embassy to full operational status without delay.

As we stood around in the darkness assessing the damage
as best we could and making sure that everyone in the compound was accounted for, I was summoned to the Niavaran
Palace. I replied firmly that I would come in my own time
when I had satisfied myself regarding the well-being of my
staff and their families. I set out about an hour later in a
decrepit Iranian army vehicle of Soviet manufacture, es-
corted by two armoured cars. One of them broke down within
a few hundred yards of the Embassy and the two remaining
vehicles crawled on at about fifteen miles an hour for the
ten-mile drive through the city. The streets were virtually
empty except for occasional groups of soldiers enforcing the
curfew. It was a terrible sight. The whole modern business
section of Tehran seemed to have been ravaged. I saw
multi-storey office buildings which had completely collapsed,
liquor stores still blazing, smouldering debris everywhere,
the skeletons of cars and buses overturned and abandoned –
a scene of dreadful desolation.

When I arrived at the palace, I moved into another world.
The soft-footed servants in their tail coats, the deferential
aides-de-camp, the sumptuous rooms were unchanged and it
was difficult to imagine that the Shah and the Empress were
citizens of the same war-torn city which I had just so painfully
traversed. I was ushered into the Shah's room; Sullivan was
already there. My temper had not been improved by the day's
events and I spoke harshly about the attack on the Embassy
and the complete and deliberate failure of the army to protect
us or indeed to prevent the wholesale devastation of central
Tehran. I formally demanded compensation for the extensive
damage which the Embassy had suffered. The Shah was full
of apologies and immediately agreed that we must be com-
pensated. He made no attempt to exculpate the extraordinary

behaviour of his armed forces. But he did not disguise the fact that all his political initiatives had collapsed and invited me to agree that, whatever we both might feel about the consequences, he now had no choice but to appoint a military Prime Minister: he had in fact given orders that General Azhari's appointment to the post would be announced the following day. Meanwhile he could assure me that the military would not permit a recurrence of today's events. I was forced to agree with him and remember saying that there was now no alternative: Tehran could not stand another November 5th. I returned around midnight to my darkened Embassy. My military vehicles had disappeared when I left the palace and I took a lift back in Sullivan's car. We parted without optimism.

The next day my senior staff and I took stock while my excellent technicians ingeniously repaired enough of the damage to put us back in communication with the outside world and to restore our electric power. All my Iranian staff without exception reported for duty as usual and the work of assessing damage, cleaning the smoke-blackened rooms and resuming normal operations began. We had many questions in our minds which needed immediate answers.

First, there was the behaviour of the armed forces. We agreed that deliberate orders must have been given to the troops to stand by and let the rioters do their worst, the object being to allow a situation to develop which would compel the Shah to appoint a military government. There could be no other explanation. The groups of rioters which had carried out the burnings had been small and could easily have been dispersed, but in all cases the soldiers merely watched and did nothing to stop them. General Azhari's remark to me on the telephone was further evidence and I picked up another indication from the sergeant in charge of the detachment which was by now guarding the Embassy. There were some signs during the morning that another attack on us might develop. I walked outside and asked the sergeant what he and his men would do. 'Never mind,' he replied with a smile, 'today I have much better orders.'

Next, who had attacked us and why? Apart from the Kuwait Airways office (an obvious target because of the refusal of the Kuwaiti government to admit Khomeini in October) our Embassy and the office of British Airways were the only foreign institutions which had come under attack. We discussed two theories and I have not to this day decided which, if either, was correct. Many of my Iranian staff believed that the attackers had been SAVAK agents and soldiers in civilian clothes. The reason? To teach us a lesson because of our opposition to military government, and, by the same token, to convince the British that it was futile to continue to press the Shah to strive for political solutions. Alternatively, we had been attacked by the same people who had been burning the rest of the city because we were the best substitute for the Americans that they could find. The American Embassy was heavily guarded and a difficult target: we were neither. Politically it was well known that we and the Americans were supporting the Shah, and the British government had made no secret of their support; it was therefore logical that a strike should be made at the softer target. Personally, and now with the benefit of hindsight, I incline to believe our first theory, namely that the attack had been the work of SAVAK and the armed forces. I hope that I do not do them an injustice.

Then, who had been responsible for the general campaign of burning and destruction? So far as we could judge there had been three separate events in Tehran on November 5th. First there had been a series of the by now normal violent and over-excited anti-Shah demonstrations. My wife, on her return on foot from the hairdresser's at about 12.30 p.m. had been caught up in one of these and for the first and only time during the revolution, accepted sanctuary in a nearby shop whose owner she knew. Secondly, there was the huge and peaceful crowd which I had seen assembling in the late morning to march in celebration of Ayatollah Taleghani's release from prison. Thirdly there were the small groups of school-children, students and young men who had carried out the main work of destruction. It was evident as we toured the city on November 6th that their discipline and selectivity had been remarkable. The damage, once the burnt-out carcasses of vehicles and litter had been cleared away, was much less than had appeared the night before. There had been no loss of life, something unbelievable to witnesses of the scenes of the previous day. The attacks on property had been carefully timed to coincide with the late lunch break when office buildings etc. were empty. Banks which stood alone had been gutted: banks with domestic apartments above them had not been touched. There had been no indiscriminate looting. The work was not that of 'mobs'. The Jewish carpet shops on Ferdowsi Street were untouched whereas adjacent banks and liquor shops had been razed. Every target had some connection with Pahlavism and modernisation, some anti-Islamic connotation. It was an amazing feat of organisation, timing and discipline. Our conclusion was that the Taleghani demonstration had been arranged by the religious leaders acting through local mosques, the crowd mainly comprising the artisan classes of south Tehran, the rank and file of the traditionalist movement. The burning had been organised, we felt, by the Mujahidin-e-Khalq (the People's Fighters), one of the extreme militant groups which had been conducting a guerilla war with SAVAK for years, perhaps in concert with the other main extremist group, the Fedayin-e-Islam (Those Who Sacrifice Themselves for the Faith) with possible assistance from the Communist (Tudeh) Party. All three had the organisation, the discipline and the cohesion to carry out such an operation. In this context we stumbled on interesting evidence that, a few days before November 5th, the secondary schools, which had been rather aimlessly demonstrating and plotting against the Shah, had been infiltrated by groups of adults who had organised and directed parties of children to burn and destroy when the time came: one schoolboy who was seen pocketing money from a burning bank was severely beaten by one of these organisers and forced to throw his little pile of loot on to the flames.

Whatever the truth might have been, my staff and I agreed on one crucial point. The desiderata of the extremists at both ends of the spectrum had paradoxically coincided. The armed forces had achieved their objective of forcing military government on the reluctant Shah. And the extreme opposition, by provoking military intervention and thus extinguishing all hope of a valid political solution which would have left the Shah's regime in situ, had achieved the necessary polarisation which would facilitate the downfall of the regime. The Shah's own phrase 'A military solution is no solution' was common currency in the Embassy that day.

During the next day or two the army succeeded in restoring a semblance of order to Tehran. They dispersed numerous demonstrations, the most tenacious being at Tehran university. A few more buildings were burnt and there was a fair amount of shooting by the armed forces. On November 6th the Shah publicly appealed for calm, assuring the people (with no sense of the irony of his words) that the days of tyranny and corruption were past; that in the future everything would be done according to the 1906 constitution; and that free elections would be held as quickly as possible.

However, the provinces remained turbulent and the strikes widened and deepened. By November 7th the oilfields were virtually closed down; bazaars and shops were shut; ministries were either on strike or working with skeleton staffs; the national airline was out and the Central Bank paralysed; a run on the commercial banks began. The military had attempted to impose censorship on the press; all the leading newspapers immediately struck, leaving only the radio and television which were being run by the army, and a few pro-government broadsheets. It was clear that the military government had failed from the outset either to restore calm to the country or to get the economy working again.

I saw the Shah on November 7th. I found him obsessed with prosecution of the anti-corruption drive. He told me that General Nassiri, the former head of SAVAK, had been arrested, as had General Khademi, the head of Iranair. General Khademi had committed suicide (in dubious circumstances: there were circumstantial rumours that he had been murdered by those sent to arrest him). There was a pause after which the Shah said that the generals wanted to arrest Hoveyda. I could not restrain myself any more. I said that the Shah knew Hoveyda and I had been personal friends for twenty years, but that this was not the reason why I felt I must speak out. He had been the Shah's Prime Minister for thirteen years. To arrest him would be to arrest the Shah, to try Hoveyda would be to try the Shah, and to condemn Hoveyda would be to condemn the Shah. There was a long silence at the end of which the Shah muttered something

100

about not liking political vendettas, and changed the subject.

I saw no point in disguising my feelings any further. I told the Shah that, if he was so concerned with anti-corruption, he should know that rumours were sweeping Tehran that the members of the Imperial Family who had already fled the country (nearly all of them) were planning to return and to resume their business activities now that the military had taken over. If there was any truth in this, I urged him not to permit it. I did not know where the truth lay, but the political fact was that everyone believed that the Pahlavi family was at the centre of corruption. If he did not like to hear this from me he could kick me out of the room, but I felt it my duty to speak plainly and indeed regretted that I had not done so earlier. The Shah did not take offence and asked me for details of the stories circulating about individual members of his family. I gave them and he assured me that none of the family would be allowed to return to Iran while the crisis lasted. (Two days later he announced that an investigation would be carried out into the business dealings and fortunes of the various princes and princesses.) As we said goodbye the Shah said that he was determined to replace the military government as soon as possible by a government of national unity. Liberalisation would continue whatever the cost and the march of history would not be halted or turned back.

When I returned to the Embassy that night, I was very anxious about Hoveyda's fate. I knew that the military hated him – he had never hidden his contempt for them – and I was sure that, once arrested, he would never re-emerge from prison alive, whether or not the regime was overthrown. The next morning I telephoned him at his small flat in north Tehran. Speaking in cryptic terms I said that I was worried that his former master was on the point of betraying him to his enemies and suggested that he should run for it while there was still time. He laughed. 'My dear Tony, I am an Iranian and I have done nothing that I am ashamed of. I have absolutely no intention of running away.' I urged him not to be a hero and emphasised the danger I felt certain he was in. 'No, let them do what they like. If it comes to a trial I shall have plenty to say. In any case I have a lot of detective stories to read and must stay where I am to finish them!' I gave up and we agreed that it would be better for both of us if I did not call on him in person. I undertook to telephone him again in a few days' time. He was arrested that night and I never saw him again, although I managed to get a long farewell letter to him in his prison shortly before I left Tehran for good in late January 1979. He was shot by Khomeini's regime a week or two afterwards and I know from eye-witnesses that he went to his death with as much bravery and insouciance as he had shown to me in our last telephone conversation.

I saw the Shah again on November 11th and learnt of further arrests of his former ministers and senior personalities: Mayor Gholamreza Nikpay, another close friend of mine, was among the number, his only crime being to have conscientiously tried to carry out the Shah's impossible orders for the modernisation of the grossly overcrowded capital – he too met his end bravely at the hands of Khomeini's executioners. He was another good and courageous man.

I then informed the Shah of the proposition which had been put to me by moderate opposition leaders on November 5th and which had been reiterated to a member of my staff on about November 9th. The Shah said that, if he thought it would benefit the country, he would leave the next day. But he was convinced that his departure would lead to anarchy. The armed forces would be leaderless and his departure would probably provoke a Latin American situation with the armed forces splitting, coup following coup in a condition of permanent instability. Ali Amini and Entezam, who were now advising him, were strongly urging him to stay. I agreed. The Shah went on to say that the refusal of the National Front to co-operate in a coalition had been a serious setback: they were hand in glove with Khomeini. I suggested that he should continue to explore civilian options, perhaps a cabinet of purely neutral figures, an idea which we had discussed before the fateful November 5th. As I saw it, this was the only hope of getting the country back to work again: there was no alternative except the collapse of the regime.

We had another round on the BBC. The Shah argued that the Persian broadcasts were helping to convince the people that the British were playing around with the opposition ('the people' obviously included himself). I lost my temper. I said that the next person who made this accusation to me would receive a very short answer. Anyone who was fool enough to believe that the British government would incur political odium by standing up for the regime in public – I supposed that I must have burnt down my own Embassy – when they were really playing games with the opposition, should be in a lunatic asylum. I thought that 'the people' who believed this did so out of a sense of shame that they could not solve their own problems – it was easier to blame the British than to face reality. Silence.

On November 12th I paid my first call on the new Prime Minister, General Gholamreza Azhari. Shrewd, humane and widely respected outside his immediate military circle, Azhari was a very different kind of officer from the heads of the three separate services. Oveissi (army) was a straight-forward soldier of the ramrod type: he must have been a good company commander. Rabii (air force) worshipped the Shah and, like Oveissi, was a firm believer in strong-arm measures. Habibollahi (navy) was similar although less boisterous and more thoughtful. Azhari's mind was subtle and conscious of the political dimensions of the crisis. He made no attempt to minimise the seriousness of the situation, particularly the strikes. His first duties would be to restore order and to get the country back to work: like the Shah he pinned exagger-ated faith on the impact of the anti-corruption campaign. We had the first of many discussions about the BBC – on familiar lines – although Azhari, perhaps as a result of my outburst to the Shah, was careful to assure me that he did not associate H.M. government with the BBC. He had no doubt of our support for the Shah and now understood that, during September and October, I had been advising him in good faith. The problem about the BBC broadcasts was that what would be accepted as normal reporting by Western listeners was interpreted differently by the Iranian audience. For example, if the BBC carried 'unconfirmed reports' of fatal casualties in such-and-such a town, this meant to the Iranian listeners that the casualties had occurred and that the government was covering them up. I defended the BBC. I told Azhari that I had discussed this type of accusation with the BBC correspondent in Tehran. He had let me read a batch of the reports he had sent over the previous few weeks. They had been perfectly fair. I suggested that Azhari should take advantage of the presence of a BBC television team to give an interview and state his case to the British people. He declined. 'If I give an interview, I shall have to say hard things about the BBC, and I do not want to do anything which might damage relations between Iran and Britain at this terrible stage in our history.'

As the month wore on my meetings with the Shah and with the Prime Minister became gloomier and gloomier. The security situation in Tehran and in the provinces worsened and violent riots became commonplace. Every day there was shooting and casualties. We estimated that, after the military takeover, at least 200 people must have been killed by the army in the following fortnight. One of the problems was that the troops had no training in crowd control and were incapable or unwilling to use the non-lethal internal security equipment such as batons and rubber bullets with which some had been issued. I remember one occasion in late November when I heard shooting close to the Embassy as I was walking from my office to the Residence for lunch. My press officer and I walked down the street to see what was happening. At the nearest intersection of streets a platoon of soldiers was deployed in a kneeling position reminiscent of pictures of the Boer War. Two small crowds were advancing up two separate streets towards the intersection. The pavements were full of passers-by, running in all directions to escape the mêlée. The soldiers were intermittently firing single shots from high velocity rifles straight into the advancing demonstrators. Both groups could easily have been dispersed by determined baton charges by troops with anti-riot equipment. But the Iranian army was behaving as though it was fighting a war against a national enemy.

The killing and cumulative strikes continued. Occasionally the government made some headway, as when the oilworkers went back to work briefly after some hundreds of arrests were made, and production returned for a few days to normal levels. But the respite was shortlived and the public services, the ministries, the press, the universities and the secondary schools were never brought under control. The Customs Service closed, thus starving the factories of their basic materials, while the factory workers (who until then had been working, if only intermittently) joined the national strike; there was nothing else for them to do. Selective power cuts plunged Tehran into darkness for some hours daily and there was nothing the government could do to prevent this. The strike in the Central Bank and in Iranair made it impossible to move cash to the provinces. Wages could not be paid. The unpaid workers joined the revolution.

Pressure began to build up against foreigners, particularly in the oilfields, and evidence accumulated that the opposition was armed. Foreign firms started to withdraw their personnel – most of their enterprises were on strike anyway – and more expatriates left as threatening telephone calls, pamphlets and notices stuck on doorposts multiplied. The houses of the American manager of the Oil Services Company in Ahwaz and of the Iranian Field Operations Manager were fire-bombed, creating more anxiety amongst the foreign community. The economy was in ruins and the Europeans and Americans whose technical expertise was so necessary to the basic infrastructure were starting to pull out or to be forced out.

The activities of the Shah and of the government assumed an air of unreality. The Shah was besieged with advisers and different advice. Everyone had his preferred solution, from government supporters to moderate opposition politicians, generally variants on the theme that the Shah must temporarily withdraw (either from Tehran or from Iran itself) in order to enable a national consensus of moderates to revive the country and hold elections. Only the tougher elements in the military favoured sterner action – mass arrests, shootings, a 'crack-down'. To his credit the Shah's views did not waver. He stuck to three main points. First, if he left the country the armed forces would split or collapse and there would be chaos. Second, the military government must be seen to be transitional to a restoration of civilian rule, probably at the end of January. Third, a strong-arm policy would precipitate the next phase of revolution, namely terrorism, sabotage and armed insurrection; and in any case a crack-down was irrelevant to the problem of the strikes which, more than the rioting and demonstrating, were draining away the life-blood of the regime.

General Azhari's policies were consonant with the Shah's views. He withdrew the top military commanders from their ministerial posts – much to their relief – and presented a mainly civilian and constitutional face to the people; he conscientiously submitted all government measures to parliamentary debate and restrained the wilder of the generals who longed to cut loose against the populace. He frequently emphasised in public the temporary nature of his government and promised a reasonably early return to civilian government. He even began mildly to enjoy his role as Prime Minister, particularly his exchanges in the parliament, although he never fell victim to unjustified optimism.

The fact was that all this manoeuvring was, as one of my Iranian friends put it to me, 'playing with words in a vacuum'. Khomeini's prestige was so high, and his simple message that the Shah must go, to be replaced by an Islamic Republic, had heightened the temper of the country to such an extent, that none of the political stratagems of the government or of the moderate opposition looked like breaking the deadlock. My feeling was that only exhaustion and widening concern about the slide to anarchy might open the way for those in the middle ground to persuade the mass of the people to accept a constitutional solution retaining the Shah, stripped of all his powers, except for those of Commander-in-Chief. But I saw no signs of this evolution beginning to germinate.

We came to the conclusion in the last days of November that the loyalty of the armed forces was finally beginning to crumble. There was no serious trouble at the top and the rank and file had held on well for a long time. But evidence was coming in of soldiers fraternising with rioters on November 5th and in some cases even helping in the destruction of buildings. Stories of desertions from units in the provinces proliferated; also of incidents where troops had fired on military helicopters and sabotaged military equipment. I put a heavy question mark over the willingness of the army to have another major round with the people unless they could be absolutely sure that the Shah would be the ultimate winner – and they could not.

Against this depressing background the authorities awaited what they knew would be their next test – the beginning of the month of Moharram (December 1st). Moharram is the holiest month in the calendar of Shi'ite Islam. It embraces the anniversaries of the martyrdoms of the two sons of the Prophet Mohammed's son-in-law and, to the Shi'ite sect, legitimate successor, Ali ibn Abi Talib. Imam Hassan, the elder son of Ali, died on the ninth day of Moharram (Ta'sua) and Imam Hossein, Ali's younger son, was killed by the forces of the Omayyad Caliph on the tenth day of Moharram (Ashura). The whole month, and in particular these two days, is given up to religious observances and mourning ceremonies. These take the form of public processions, services at mosques and at specially prepared pavilions, passion plays and rites involving self-flagellation with chains. It is a period when emotions run high throughout Shi'ite Islam and, given the powerful religious drive behind the movement against the Shah, it was an obvious time for a decisive push against the tottering structure of the regime.

On November 22nd Khomeini issued instructions from Paris for the tactics to be used during Moharram. He directed the people to hold their ceremonies in defiance of bans from the authorities. The people should go into the streets to express the true evil of the regime. Theological students should go to the countryside to ensure that the farmers and villagers understood that the clergy stood for the revival of agriculture and not for the handover of the land to its previous owners – a shrewd move to cover the mullahs' weak flank, the Shi'ite Church having been a substantial land-owner before the Shah's land reforms. Finally Khomeini ominously described Moharram as a month of blood and vengeance.

My state of mind at the end of November was one of unrelieved pessimism. As I had anticipated, the people had reacted to the military government by an almost total withdrawal of co-operation – the strikes – and the military were incapable of getting the country back to work. The armed forces were shaky and the earlier demands for the restoration of the constitution had been drowned by Khomeini's cry of 'Death to the Shah!' and the establishment of an Islamic Republic. The military could not even keep order in the streets. The political manoeuvres of the Shah and his advisers, of the moderate opposition, indeed of the government itself, seemed to me to be a play of shadows, divorced from the hard realities of the revolutionary movement. If it was a question of stamina, of which side could hold out longest, as Sharif-Emami had said to me what seemed like years ago, all the evidence pointed in one direction, that the opposition were winning this battle. We waited for what Moharram would bring.

December 1978–January 1979

We did not have to wait long. The government had issued instructions that there would be no public processions, that religious ceremonies would be confined to the mosques and that there would be a curfew in the streets at 9 p.m. every evening. The month of Moharram formally began at sundown on December 1st. That day, strange though it may seem, my wife and I went to the races. The Tehran racecourse was newly opened and was one of the few institutions in the city which was not on strike. There was a fair crowd present, a cross-section of the population, and we had a pleasant day. We returned to the Embassy at nightfall through quiet streets. Punctually at 9 p.m. huge demonstrations erupted throughout the city, particularly in the area of the bazaar. In the streets and from the rooftops the people defied the government edicts. The army responded vigorously and, until about midnight, there was a tempest of machine-gun and rifle fire, even shots from the heavy guns on the tanks, interspersed with wild bursts of 'Allahu Akbar!' (God is greatest) from the rebellious people of Tehran. We stood in the darkness (the electricity workers had cut the power supply again) at the gate of the Embassy listening to these astonishing surges of sound. The section of soldiers guarding us were nervous and the young officer in command had a fainting fit. Occasionally a tank would clatter past on the way to the bazaar. I recall remarking to my wife that General Gordon would have recognised the scene from his last days in Khartoum.

The next day the military controlled radio admitted that seven people had been killed (they subsequently increased the figure), with twenty-four wounded and a hundred put under arrest. After comparing notes with our diplomatic colleagues and others we assessed the dead at nearer to 500. Pamphlets with this figure for the 'martyrs of the 1st of Moharram' were in circulation before the day was out. There was a demand for a one-day general strike: everything closed.

Night after night the same pattern repeated itself. At 9 p.m. large crowds gathered in the streets and on the roofs, shouting 'Allahu Akbar!' and defying the troops. The soldiers fired off millions of rounds of ammunition, mostly in the air. Generally all was quiet by midnight although I remember being woken with a violent start one night at about 2 a.m. by the shattering crack of a tank gun being loosed off – God knows what at – just outside the Embassy compound. By day small groups of militant demonstrators roamed the streets, disrupting any semblance of normal life and clashing with the soldiers. On December 3rd, a large bomb exploded at one of the central police stations, destroying it. Within two or three days the credibility of the military government had been almost entirely eroded by the universal and successful defiance of the people.

There was little that General Azhari could do. He closed all schools until after Ashura and repeatedly called for calm, blaming the demonstrations on the 'enemies of the country', his code word for the Tudeh (Communist) Party whose leader had announced from Moscow in November the party's support for Khomeini and the National Front. But the disturbances continued and the strike situation got worse.

Khomeini had already spoken, on December 2nd. In a communiqué issued from Paris he called on all soldiers to leave their barracks and the service of the oppressors and to unite with the people. He gave thanks for the general strike and ordered the strikes to continue in order to paralyse the government. Any politician who planned to form a government under the traitor Shah should be rejected and regarded as an opponent of Islam.

Ta'sua (December 10th) and Ashura (December 11th) drew near. By this time the nightly shoutings and shootings had declined and it was possible to attach some credence to the government propaganda line that, after the first few days, most people had stayed at home and that the nightly noises of the crowds, the shouts of 'Allahu Akbar!' and the volleys of shots were in reality amplified tape recordings played through the loudspeakers of the mosques: anything can happen in Iran! After a number of changes of mind, all of which were quickly rumoured throughout the city, the government decided to rescind its ban on processions in order to allow the Ta'sua and Ashura marches to take place; the troops would be withdrawn from the streets to an east-west line north of the main procession route, in order to minimise provocation. In the circumstances, I was sure that General Azhari was right. His concessions were interpreted as weakness but the alternative would have been either a bloodbath of unprecedented proportions, or the immediate and final collapse of the armed forces.

The two great processions on Ta'sua and Ashura respectively were awe-inspiring in their scale, orderliness and unity of purpose. The British Embassy is situated overlooking Ferdowsi Street, one of the tributary roads leading from south Tehran to the main east-west road which bisects the centre of the city, the route for the processions which culminated at Shahyad Square close to the airport, some five miles from central Tehran. From 9 a.m. until lunchtime on each morning I stood at my window while serried ranks of marchers passed up Ferdowsi Street on their way to join the processions. The street is wide but it was filled from pavement to pavement and from top to bottom as far as the eye could see for a period of three or four hours. And it was only one of many feeder roads to the main procession route. The popular estimate of one to one and a half million people on each day cannot have been an exaggeration. Every group had its banners and its slogans. 'Death to the butcher Shah', 'Islamic Republic', and 'Khomeini is our leader' were the commonest although there were anti-American and even one or two anti-Soviet banners. For the first time the radical organisations, the Mujahidin and the Fedayin, marched openly under their flags. For the great part the demonstrators were the artisan and bazaar class of Tehran and their families. This was no half-starved rabble from shanty towns. Well dressed, healthy, the women carrying babies or leading children by the hand, the backbone of traditional, urban Iranian society passed before our eyes in their thousands. They took little notice of the watching British diplomats except for the occasional, quite friendly wave; there was no hostility, only a roar of laughter in which we joined when one man shouted out, 'British Ambassador, go home!' It was a sight which I shall never forget and it brought home to me how wise the authorities had been not to try to prevent the marches taking place or, even worse, to disperse them by force. Either course was unthinkable. There was not a soldier or a policeman to be seen anywhere – the crowds were organised, and brilliantly organised, by their own marshals – and I concealed our Embassy guard of about ten Iranian soldiers inside the building. They were happy to withdraw from public view and made only one demand – the provision of a radio set on which they could receive the BBC Persian service!

On the second day – Ashura – the temper of the marchers was more militant and there were rumours of serious violence in the provinces. As the crowds dispersed in the evening, groups of them swept through the street shouting, 'Death to the Shah!' and a dangerous riot seemed imminent; it did not materialise. However we soon learnt that the SAVAK headquarters in Shiraz had been attacked and that off-duty soldiers had joined the Shiraz marchers. Statues of the Shah's father had been pulled down in many towns. Most serious, there had been a shoot-out at the headquarters of the Imperial Iranian Ground Forces in Tehran on December 11th. Some soldiers had burst into an officers' mess and opened up with automatic fire. Seven officers of the Imperial Guard had been killed and nearly fifty wounded. Further rumours came in of desertions from the garrison at Mashhad and the sabotage of aircraft by air force technicians at Tabriz.

And the opposition had united as never before. At the climax of the Ashura procession, a mullah had read out a seventeen-point declaration on behalf of all opposition groups and parties, each specified by name. The main points

111

in the declaration were that Khomeini was the leader and all his commands would be obeyed; the regime must be overthrown; the strikes must be supported; and the army must combine with the people. The remainder read like the detailed manifesto of an incoming government.

The immediate consequences of the Ashura marches were drastic. The Tehran mullahs who had organised the marches so successfully had strengthened their position in relation to the more moderate mullahs of Qom and Mashhad. The political (as opposed to religious) opposition groups, by their association with the seventeen-point declaration, had secured some of the mass support which they had hitherto lacked. Most crucially, the military government could no longer even pretend to be in control of the country: the defiance of their authority had been so massive and so successful that it could now be said that, if there was a government at all, it comprised the power of the masses, directed by Khomeini through the network of the religious structure throughout Iran.

On December 13th, there was a rush of so-called spontaneous pro-government rallies in the provinces. In Isfahan, in Mashhad, in Arak and elsewhere, busloads of villagers invaded the streets. They were joined by soldiers. The windows of shops and offices carrying posters of Khomeini were smashed and people were forced at gunpoint to shout, 'Long live the Shah!' The opposition mobilised its forces and the two waves of demonstrations clashed, leaving many dead. General Azhari was furious. He told me a few days later that all the good done by the restraint shown by the armed forces over Ashura had been dissipated by these outbreaks. The pro-Shah demonstrations had been arranged by local commanders and the situation had got much worse as a result. The general strike had resumed and great bitterness and emotion had been generated in areas which had hitherto been relatively peaceful. The unity of the military chain of command had been broken and Azhari had issued orders that any individual commander who acted on his own initiative in such a way would be immediately dismissed and court-martialled – General Naji, Commander of the Isfahan Garrison, was dismissed a few days later.

At the Niavaran Palace the Shah pursued his desperate

attempts to put together a civilian coalition or neutral government to take over from the military if the security and strike situation ever permitted. He had for some weeks been in touch with Sadeghi, a former minister in Mossadegh's government who had subsequently severed his connections with the National Front. On December 19th the Shah told me that Sadeghi had agreed to form a government on four conditions. There must be strict adherence to the 1906 constitution. If he succeeded in forming a cabinet, it must first be approved by both houses of parliament. Control of the police and the gendarmerie must be vested in the Minister of the Interior. SAVAK's internal role must be transferred to the police, leaving SAVAK responsible only for countering external threats to Iran. The Shah had accepted these conditions. Sadeghi had further insisted on the lifting of martial law and the freeing of the press; he would negotiate the return to work of the schools and universities after he became Prime Minister. Finally he had asked the Shah for two weeks to conduct consultations on the above programme.

According to the Shah, Ali Amini had been advising him in a different sense. He had concluded that the Shah should withdraw to Bandarabbas, the Iranian port at the southern outlet of the Persian Gulf, handing over to a Council of Monarchy which would fulfil all the Shah's functions except that of Commander-in-Chief: this would remain with the Shah. Thereafter a national government, presumably under Amini's premiership, would be formed. The Shah had also seen Sanjabi, I think for the only time. Sanjabi had said that there could be no solution without a green light from Khomeini. This would be impossible to secure without the Shah's abdication.

The Shah and I agreed that Sadeghi's chances of success were slender, to say the least, and that Amini's plan was a non-starter. I said that Sadeghi would have no chance unless he could be assured that the religious leaders and the bazaars were prepared to acquiesce to the extent of calling on the people to give the new government a chance. This possibility seemed remote. Khomeini would go flat out to destroy Sadeghi. With a free press and the troops back in their barracks, I thought that the situation could pass completely out of control in a few days. In my observation, the army was showing the strain and getting ragged: divisions were appearing between hawks and doves in the higher ranks. I doubted whether, once martial law had been lifted and the troops had returned to their camps, it would be possible to get them out again if the security situation so required.

The Shah was inclined to agree. He had considerable doubts about Sadeghi and was disposed to accept Sanjabi's more realistic view. The armed forces would accept the Sadeghi plan if he, the Shah, assured them that it would work. But how could he? As regards Amini's idea, the army would disintegrate if he withdrew. There might even be a coup to prevent him from leaving Tehran and he would become the puppet of a military junta; there would certainly be a coup after he left. Such ideas were unthinkable.

Although the Shah was by now almost entirely without hope of a successful outcome to the crisis and discussed the elaborate schemes of his advisers and interlocutors with smiling irony and a good deal of scepticism, he was showing no sign of throwing in the sponge or of physical or mental deterioration. On the contrary his manner was calm and realistic and he maintained that the only solution, if one existed, lay in free elections and the full implementation of the 1906 constitution; the clock could not be put back and the iron fist was neither practicable nor desirable – 'A dictator may survive by slaughtering his people, a king cannot act in such a way.' I did not doubt his sincerity and I believed that he was now – tragically too late – close to common ground with the liberally minded, democratic political forces in his country. But the crisis had resolved itself into an all-out battle between Khomeini and the masses on one side and the Shah and the armed forces on the other, for the public voice of the middle ground was lost in the clamour. In any case the National Front was so suspicious of the Shah's duplicity that all their solutions involved his physical withdrawal from the scene; otherwise they feared that, if they co-operated and the country returned to normal, he would immediately double-cross them, resume his autocratic ways and clap them all in jail. It was hopeless.

On my part, I continued to believe that the only chance,

tenuous and almost non-existent though it might be, was for the Shah to persist in his search for a political solution through Sadeghi. I agreed with the Shah that his withdrawal would precipitate a series of debilitating military coups or the disintegration of the armed forces. But we were getting close to the bottom of the barrel. If the Shah stayed and Sadeghi, the last chance, failed, there would be no alternative to the worst outcome – the continuation of the deadly war of attrition leading to economic ruin and a legacy of bitterness and extremism haunting an unstable and unreliable Iran for many years.

In the middle of the month there were stirrings outside the group of politicians who were now directly in touch with the Shah. Some moderate religious leaders revived the idea of the Shah leaving the country temporarily while a Regency Council, now to include both military officers (in order to placate the armed forces) and National Front politicians, prepared the way for elections. This initiative even got so far, according to my information, as a proposal that Ayatollahs Rafsanjani and Montazeri, both known to be Khomeini men, should visit Paris to try to sell the idea to the old gentleman. It was suggested that my American colleague and I should act as intermediaries with the Shah. But the idea fizzled out before it took hold when the two ayatollahs, disillusioned and shocked by the pro-Shah violence mounted by the local military commanders in the provinces, refused to make the trip. Another glimmer of hope was extinguished.

On December 18th I had my first intimation that Shapour Bakhtiar, one of the leaders of the National Front, French educated and a long-term opponent of the Shah, was contemplating a bid for the Prime Ministry. We lunched together that day at the house of a mutual friend and had a doom-laden discussion about the situation. Bakhtiar was pessimistic. He said that Khomeini must be defused and the Shah must give cast-iron guarantees of future good conduct before any serious politician would co-operate in forming a government. The Shah must withdraw in order to give a new cabinet the free hand it would need to restore order and revive the economy. But he could see the danger that the army would divide or collapse if the Shah left the country. Bakhtiar gave no direct hint that he would accept the Prime Ministry but I sensed that this was in his mind. I told him that anyone who took on the job would be a brave man. Personally I doubted whether it would be possible for a new Prime Minister to resolve the crisis if he had been formally appointed by the Shah: anti-Shah feeling was running far too high and I had in the last few days come to doubt whether Sadeghi had any chance of success. It was a friendly but inconclusive discussion.

On December 21st General Azhari had a heart attack. Being a courageous and patriotic man, he concealed the fact from the public, working on and living in his office at the Prime Ministry. But he was in despair. The news of the Sadeghi plan had destroyed the morale of his cabinet who were unwilling to continue with their impossible tasks once they knew that the Shah was planning to replace them. Azhari believed that the morale of the armed forces was on a downward slide. If the Sadeghi plan failed, there would be more political manoeuvres and further deterioration of military morale; the Shah's indecision was destroying the will of his generals. If martial law was lifted, Azhari had no doubt that it would be impossible for it to be reimposed. I could not but agree with this bleak analysis. The various military commanders were beginning openly to criticise the Shah and to compare his performance unfavourably with that of his father. Senior officers started to send their families away to Europe or the United States.

On December 22nd, Sullivan and I had another long meeting with the Shah. He told us that Sadeghi would report on the outcome of his consultations on December 25th. If he succeeded in forming a government and the situation in the streets got out of control, there would be a military crackdown. There was no choice between that and unconditional surrender. But he, the Shah, could not associate himself with such action by the military. If it had to come, he would retire to Bandarabbas 'to visit my navy'. Did I see any alternative to this course of action?

I repeated what I had said before, namely that Sadeghi would have no chance unless the religious and bazaar leaders were prepared to call on the people to stay calm and give the new government a chance. Without such a guarantee, the situation would slip out of control immediately. I asked the Shah if, in such circumstances, the army would be able and willing to mount a crack-down. The Shah said that he had no idea and asked for my opinion. I replied that my inner feeling was that the army might split – the troops might do their duty in certain areas and refuse to in others. This would be a disaster which could lead to civil war.

The Shah continued that, if Sadeghi failed to form a government, there was no choice but to carry on with Azhari, or with another military Prime Minister if Azhari was not physically fit, until Now Ruz (the Persian New Year festival which starts on March 21st and continues for thirteen days, normally a period of relaxation for the whole country) in the hope that continuing attrition would weaken the opposition more than the armed forces.

The Shah was more resolute and determined in his manner than he had been for some time. He appeared to be in no frame of mind to contemplate any of the propositions involving his departure from the country which were being canvassed by the liberal opposition factions. But the options, as the three of us agreed, were becoming very thin and unconvincing.

On December 23rd there was a marked turn for the worse. In Ahwaz the American Field Manager of the Oil Services Company was shot down on his way to his office, precipitating an exodus of expatriate staff from the oilfields. In Tehran, the secondary schools reopened and there was a fresh wave of violent demonstrations: the cry of 'Death to the Shah!' echoed in the city streets, punctuated by firing. On December 24th the riots spread and there was an attack on the American Embassy. The military guard took no action and the attackers were repelled by the US Marine Corps security personnel, firing tear gas, but not before the main gate had been breached and a car burnt. My wife and I were fortuitous witnesses of this assault. I was due to leave Tehran shortly on transfer to a new appointment as deputy to the Permanent Under-Secretary at the FCO. We had arranged to pay our farewell call on the Empress on December 24th. In the surrealistic atmosphere of illusory normality which still surrounded life in Tehran, we were obliged to wear formal dress – a morning coat for me and a hat and long gloves for my wife. We successfully dodged the demonstrators on our way to the palace but stuck fast in an impenetrable traffic jam on our return. We were only a few hundred yards from our own Embassy and about 200 yards west of the American Embassy. After sitting for a time in the car while a confused mob of demonstrators and passers-by surged around in the street between us and our destination, we decided that we had better walk the remaining distance. I was tempted to stride down the street in my top hat and morning coat, but thought that this might be regarded as frivolous by the intense young men who were delivering pavement speeches all round us. My wife threw her elaborate hat into the back of the car and I put on the coat which my plain-clothes policeman was wearing. Thus, in semi-formal dress, we walked back to our house. I remember seeing a small crowd trying to break into the American Embassy as we passed, and I noticed the tear gas canisters flying over the wall to meet them. No one showed any hostility towards us and I recall one young man walking beside us and saying, in English, 'This is horribly important.' I agreed with him.

Our parting with the Empress had been melancholy. She was composed but curiously detached. I remember her describing the burning of Tehran on November 5th as 'a little *feu de joie* by the people', a description which seemed inadequate to those of us who had spent that day in the business quarter of the city. Politically she felt there was nothing the West could do to help to resolve the crisis, and indeed she suggested that the open support expressed for the Shah by the British and American governments might by now be damaging to the regime. As we were about to leave, I asked her on a purely personal basis how I could get in touch with Hoveyda in prison. I said that I could not leave Iran without doing so. I could not help him but I owed it to our long friendship at least to say goodbye, and I knew that he had always been very close to the Empress. She appeared uninterested and scarcely concerned about Hoveyda's fate.

The bad times continued. Every day small crowds of rioters tested the armed forces by burning car tyres and rubbish in the streets in widely separated areas, and there was more shooting. The provinces were seething with unrest and the revolutionaries were set to take over some of the main provincial cities. There was a horrifying clash between the army and the people in Mashhad where, after a day of rioting and heavy firing by the garrison, the soldiers were forced to retreat to their barracks. The strikes went on and oil production dropped far below domestic demand. Long queues for petrol and kerosene formed in Tehran, monitored by soldiers whose way of keeping order was to fire bursts of automatic fire into the air. My wife and I decided that we had better abandon another feature of our normal life – skiing. It was becoming difficult to get enough petrol for the one-hour drive to the superb resort of Dizin in the Elburz Mountains, north of Tehran. The last time we skied, just before or after Christmas, the slopes were moderately full of Iranian and foreign skiers. At the bottom of the ski-lift there was a surly group of local mullahs and villagers, watched by a platoon of gendarmerie; there were rumours of bombs having been placed in the lifts, an uncomfortable thought. I went up in the gondola for the last time with a young Iranian ski-instructor who had been educated in England. Neither of us pretended that there was any hope for the future, and he told me that the resort was closing: it was becoming too dangerous.

But we had an agreeable Christmas in the Embassy, with the added romance of candlelight because of the daily electricity cuts by the striking power workers. It was just possible to buy presents from the occasional open shop and the strikers saw to it that there were no serious shortages of food in the city. The Christian churches in Tehran held their Christmas services unmolested and life was not so terrible that I hesitated to bring my twelve-year-old daughter out from England for the Christmas holidays.

At the end of another bad day of rioting and heavy firing on December 28th, the Foreign Minister told me that Sadeghi had asked for another six weeks for consultations. We agreed that this eliminated him from the contest. I also gathered that furious intrigues were developing around the Niavaran Palace. Ardeshir Zahedi, Iranian Ambassador in Washington, was back in Tehran and was being hyper-active, advocating strong government and a military crack-down and letting it be understood that he was acting with the knowledge and authority of Brzezinski. Zahedi was an unashamed activist and loyalist, the son of the General Zahedi who had toppled Mossadegh in 1953 and himself a veteran of those events: a powerful man who had once been married to the Shah's eldest daughter and had served as Ambassador in London and as Foreign Minister before his appointment to Washington. I had more faith in his zeal than in his judgment.

I assessed the situation in the darkest terms at the end of the year. The country was grinding down rapidly to anarchy. Cities, towns and villages were in an uproar and effective government had ceased to exist. The strikes were holding firm and Mehdi Bazargan, of whom more hereafter, was in the oilfields, with the authority of the Qom ayatollahs and allegedly of Khomeini as well, trying to negotiate a restoration of oil production to meet internal demand; the strikers were now out of the control of the opposition leadership. On December 30th the British Council centres in Ahwaz, Shiraz and Mashhad, as well as the American and Turkish Consulates in Tabriz, had been attacked and severely damaged. In Ahwaz the military had temporarily lost control of the city, as they had permanently lost control in Mashhad.

Into this confused situation, Shapour Bakhtiar had suddenly emerged as the next candidate for the Prime Ministry. This move had split the National Front but Bakhtiar, in conversation with me, was firm and confident. He told me that the Shah had agreed to leave the country for rest or medical treatment; that a Regency Council would be appointed; and that the command of the armed forces would be vested in the cabinet. I could not share his optimism or that of those others who were promoting his cause. He had been rejected by the National Front leaders and I believed that Khomeini would easily brush him aside. I could not envisage Bakhtiar, with all his courage and resolution but without any political constituency, being able to restore order and break the strikes even if the Shah withdrew after the new government was confirmed.

My view was that the Shah's withdrawal could only have the desired effect, although even this was incredibly unlikely, if it became the means of bringing into play a broad enough range of political and religious personalities – not a rejected single member of the National Front – to have a chance of calming the people down and getting the economy back to work. In such circumstances, even if the Shah's withdrawal became permanent, the transition to a republic would at least be controlled. But I could no longer see how this could happen. Apart from Bakhtiar, and given that the neutral caretaker alternative had died with Sadeghi, I saw three further options, all of them counsels of despair. Azhari could, if he was fit enough, continue the war of attrition. But the oil crisis made this impossible – the paralysis of the country could not continue for another three months of the bitter Iranian winter. Azhari could be replaced by a stronger general – there was talk of General Djam, former Chief of Staff and now living in England, but he was obviously and wisely reluctant to enter the fray. But I did not believe that a tougher policy adopted by a sterner military Prime Minister would bring about even a temporary improvement. Or alternatively there could be a full takeover by a military junta in the Shah's name with the Shah withdrawing from Tehran to, say, Bandarabbas. This would in my view be the worst of all options, leading probably to disintegration of the armed forces or to civil war.

On December 31st it was officially announced that Bakhtiar would form a government and that the Shah would go overseas for rest and medical attention. Ardeshir Zahedi continued to deny that there was any question of the Shah leaving the country and, so far as I knew at the time, Zahedi was still advocating a tough, military policy. The Americans too were becoming active albeit, as I judged, with divided counsels. The general belief, fostered by Zahedi, was that the White House staff, led by Brzezinski, was in favour of a military crack-down, whatever that meant, whereas the State Department and Sullivan believed that there must be a political solution and were disposed to support Bakhtiar. Some time in early January General Huyser, Deputy Commander of NATO Forces, arrived, with the task, as I understood it, of persuading the generals not to carry out a coup but to support Bakhtiar after the Shah's withdrawal. I was not privy to these bewildering intrigues and counter-intrigues and can only speak from hearsay. But I recommended to London that we should keep clear of these dangerous and futile cross-currents. I had no further constructive advice to offer the Shah, for I was convinced that neither of the courses under consideration – a Bakhtiar government or tough military action – had the remotest chance of success, and I had come to the conclusion, with its obvious connotation, that the strikes which were killing the country and effectively precluding any return to normality would not break so long as the Shah was in Iran. Overall I believed that we were faced with a peculiarly Iranian crisis and that the only hope was for the Iranians to work it out for themselves, whatever the result. I believed that American or British meddling would do nothing but harm. Neither we nor the Americans were in a position to know with any certainty the consequences of any course of action which we might advocate and we would only get the blame if things went wrong. I therefore recommended that I should discontinue my talks with the Shah unless I was actually summoned to the palace, for if I saw him, I would have to speak in terms of my utterly pessimistic analysis, and this would merely heighten the Shah's paranoid suspicions of British plotting and do no good. London agreed and for the next week I maintained close touch with my remaining influential contacts, including Bakhtiar, but kept away from the Niavaran Palace.

The grim procession to disaster rolled on. On January 1st the south-western towns of Dezful and Andimeshk exploded and the army was forced to retreat. Bazargan was having no success in persuading the oilworkers to increase production and the queues for kerosene, the staple fuel for cooking and heating, grew longer. (Strangely, normal Persian indiscipline gave way in these queues to astonishing orderliness and civic spirit. After a time, when the situation deteriorated to the point where it took a day to reach the head of a queue, the modus operandi was adopted of roping the hundreds of plastic containers together; the man at the pump filled one and pulled the rope, bringing the next one forward. The owners of the containers could thus go away and return when they judged that their containers would be nearing the pump.

There was no queue jumping and little or no disorder – a unique scene.) It was around this time that General Azhari formally resigned, leaving the country without a government, even in name. In spite of gathering rumours, Zahedi continued to deny that the Shah would leave.

A witch-hunt started against SAVAK and the SAVAK headquarters in Shiraz was sacked; some officers were killed by the mob; expatriate houses in the south were firebombed; and the cities of Qazvin and Tabriz erupted with heavy casualties. General Oveissi left for the United States on January 4th, to be replaced by General Najemi, and General Qarabaghi, who had been at the military college with the Shah and had served as Minister of the Interior under Azhari, was appointed Chief of Staff. On January 8th General Azhari, genuinely in need of medical treatment, left the country. Without knowing it, he and his colleagues had dealt themselves an impossible hand when they had obliged the Shah to bring in a military government on November 5th. Azhari had done his best and now he had gone, following Sharif-Emami into the shadows.

On January 6th Bakhtiar presented his cabinet to the Shah. The latter made a brief statement to the effect that he was tired of the burden of responsibility and needed a rest. This might take place outside Iran.

Meanwhile I was preparing to leave Tehran. I had agreed with London that I would return as soon as it was felt that I could be of no further use. I would stay until the Shah left, if indeed he decided to go quickly, and until I was satisfied that the bulk of the British community had departed and that there was no one left in control of practical matters, such as the functioning of the airport for evacuating British subjects, with whom I had personal influence. We provisionally fixed on January 21st for my departure, following another vast march which was due to take place on January 19th, the fortieth day after Ashura.

Between January 6th and 16th my assessment remained unchanged. Bakhtiar's policy statements, although admirable in content, were ignored and I detected no sign that he was picking up political momentum. The delay in the Shah's departure was eroding any vestigial chance that Bakhtiar might have of gaining the confidence of the people. This delay was caused, as I thought, by two factors – first by the insistence of Zahedi and the hard-line generals that the Shah should not leave, and secondly by the absurdly legalistic and irrelevant view of the Shah and Bakhtiar that the Shah must stay until Bakhtiar's government was confirmed by the two houses of parliament – as if anyone in the streets was displaying the remotest interest in the activities of the parliament. The military were losing control of the provinces, although at a heavy cost in civilian lives, and 'people's power' was moving in to replace them – Shiraz fell on January 11th, two days after martial law there had been lifted. Even in Tehran the police had disappeared and traffic was being directed, rather efficiently, by young civilians. Food and fuel for the poor in the cities, including Tehran, was being distributed by the mosques, not by the authorities. The demonstrators were ardently wooing the soldiers in the streets and the possibility of the army taking tough, co-ordinated action against them seemed remote. In brief I was witnessing a classic revolutionary situation. The King was in the process of being dethroned. Army loyalty was uncertain and unfocused. Constituted government could not gain respect for its writ. The mass of the people were exuberant, but extremists lurked in the wings ready to direct the masses to their own purposes.

I called on the Shah to say goodbye on January 8th. I found him calm and detached, talking about events as though they no longer had relevance to him as a person. It was for me a profoundly emotional experience. I had come to know the Shah well over the previous five years and we had become intimate through the many long discussions which we had had over the four months of his ultimate travail. I started by saying that I had never imagined myself saying goodbye to him in such tragic circumstances and that I was finding it difficult to speak. I suggested that we should part without further ceremony or discussion: I would find another long session unbearable. The Shah smiled and put his hand on my arm as I dried up, literally with tears in my eyes. 'Never mind, I know how you feel. But we must have one last talk.' He told me that he was still receiving three conflicting sets of advice. Some people were telling him that he must stay and 'tough it out'. Others were saying that he should withdraw to Bandarabbas and let the army do the job in his absence. Others were advising him to leave the country. What did I think? I replied that I would prefer not to answer. Whatever I said would be construed by him as a British plot, and I had no comfort to offer. The Shah insisted. I said that I would only reply if he gave me his word of honour that he would accept what I said as my personal view, the opinion of someone who wished him and his country well, and that I was not speaking in any sense to a brief from London. The Shah accepted these conditions.

I told him that I saw him in what the Americans would describe as a 'no-win' situation. To borrow one of his metaphors, Bakhtiar was melting like snow in water every day that the Shah stayed in the country. But if he left I could see little or no possibility of his ever returning; I had no faith in Bakhtiar's ability to restore the situation. As regards the other choices, he knew what I felt about military crack-downs. I did not believe that such action was possible, and after all, it was really the strikes which had brought the regime to its knees: could the military 'crack down' on every house in the country and oblige its occupants to return to work? The Bandarabbas idea I dismissed out of hand. If the revolutionaries forced him to withdraw that far, would they not redouble their efforts to force him the whole way?

With a strange gesture the Shah looked at his watch. 'If it was up to me, I would leave in – ten minutes.' He went on to say that he could not leave before Bakhtiar was confirmed by parliament. If he left before that process was complete, parliament might collapse and there would be no quorum. I told him that Iran was in the middle of a cataclysmic revolution – no one cared about the parliament and its procedures. They had all been swept aside. The Shah shook his head and we then discussed where he should go when he left the country. He did not appear to have made up his mind and said something to the effect that he might go to 'one of those Arab kingdoms'. No mention of Egypt but he did say that he could not come to Britain: the security problem would be too acute with tens of thousands of Iranian students in the country.

We turned to the past. Why, the Shah asked, had the

people turned against him after all that he had done for them? I said that we had discussed this many times before. I thought that the basic reason was that he had tried to turn the people of Iran into something which they were not, and they had at last rebelled under the leadership of their traditional authorities, the religious classes. It was interesting that the same forces which had humbled Nasruddin Shah in 1892 when he had awarded a tobacco concession to a foreign firm, and had prevailed over Muzafferiddin Shah in 1906 over the constitution, had combined to bring down Mohammed Reza Shah – the mullahs, the bazaar and the intelligentsia. I had never admired the Iranian people as much as I had done in the past few months. Their courage, discipline and devotion to the cause of overthrowing the monarchy had been amazing; if only he had been able to mobilise these qualities in his pursuit of the Great Civilisation ... The Shah agreed about the performance of his people but rejected my analogies with his Qajar predecessors. 'I have done more for Iran than any Shah for 2,000 years; you cannot compare me to those people.'

He saw me to the door with his usual courtesy and I wished him luck whatever happened. He smiled and said nothing. I never saw him again.

Bakhtiar's cabinet and programme were approved by parliament on January 16th and the Shah, accompanied by the Empress, left Mehrabad airport for Egypt the same day. At 2 p.m. local time the radio announced the Shah's departure. My wife and I and my staff and their families were in the Embassy compound. Immediately the whole city erupted in a paroxysm of joy and release. Bursts of car horns, flashing headlights, shouting, dancing in the street, fraternisation with the soldiers, distribution of newspapers with huge banner headlines declaring 'The Shah has gone', the pulling down of statues of the Shah and his father – these are some of the things I remember from a long afternoon and evening of irrepressible and seemingly inexhaustible jubilation. It was unforgettable and untinged with ill-humour. We stood at the gates of the Embassy and were waved to and given newspapers by the ebullient groups of passers-by. Our military guard wisely submitted with smiles to their armoured car becoming a platform for speakers and their rifles being

choked with flowers. I have never experienced anything quite
like it.

But this joyous release of passion did not break the tension.
On January 17th we woke to realise that the strikes were still
on, the shops closed, and there were demonstrations in the
streets. One or two ministers resigned from Bakhtiar's cabinet and the Regency Council began to fall apart: the parliamentary deputies and senators started to drift away to their
homes. That afternoon we heard the news that half a battalion
of troops had broken loose in Ahwaz. Accompanied by Chieftain tanks they had raged through the streets of the city
shooting indiscriminately and shouting, 'Long live the Shah!'
and 'The Shah must return!' Civilian casualties were heavy.

On January 19th the Arbain march took place in Tehran.
As had been the case on Ashura and Ta'sua, well over a
million people took part in the orderly, disciplined procession
to the Shahyad Monument near the airport, now the rostrum
of the revolution. The armed forces made no attempt to
interfere. At the Monument the leaders of the opposition,
including Ayatollah Taleghani and Sanjabi, issued a Ten-
Point Declaration. This stated that the Pahlavi regime was
and always had been illegitimate and that the Shah had been
overthrown; an Islamic Republic must be established and
Khomeini was invited to introduce an Islamic Revolutionary
Council and a provisional government as soon as possible;
Bakhtiar's government should not be recognised since it had
been appointed by an illegal monarch and confirmed by the
vote of an illegal parliament; the army was asked not to isolate
itself from the nation and not to allow itself to be used as an
instrument of threat and suppression; the strikes and demonstrations must continue until the final aims of the revolution
had been achieved.

On January 20th I sent my last assessment to London. I
judged that Bakhtiar's government had yet to gain a vestige
of popular support and that it was unable to govern. Khomeini's influence was supreme. There was no sign of softening
of the revolutionary line and the shutdown of economic
activity was holding. It was likely that Khomeini would
proclaim the composition of an Islamic Revolutionary
Council and a provisional government. His return would

sweep Bakhtiar away. Any day the ludicrous situation might come about that there would be two governments in Iran, Khomeini's ministers being allowed by the 'Action Committees' in each ministry to enter their offices while Bakhtiar's ministers would be barred.

Although it was faintly encouraging that the vast crowds in Tehran had been reasonably good-humoured since the departure of the Shah, this had not helped Bakhtiar: he was ignored as the cries went up of 'Death to the Shah!' and 'Khomeini is our leader!' There was no doubt what the mass of the people wanted – Khomeini and an Islamic Republic. I could not see how Bakhtiar and the armed forces could stand against this tide and it was difficult to see how the transition could take place without bloodshed and chaos. The key lay with the armed forces. The generals had acquiesced in the Shah's withdrawal on condition that the 1906 constitution be implemented, including the monarchy, thus retaining the Shah as Head of State and Commander-in-Chief. If there was a transition to an Islamic Republic the army might try to react – two armoured units (in Ahwaz and later in Dezful) had already broken ranks and savaged the people. There could be a split and a civil war.

I concluded that a Republic was inevitable and that the only way to defuse the crisis without violence would be for Khomeini and the generals to get together and for the latter to transfer their allegiance: the revolution had won and this would provide a chance for the country to be saved. Meanwhile there was no constituted government in the cities which had gone over to people's power under religious leadership. There were also the first indications of centrifugal forces getting to work. The cry of 'Arabistan' had been heard in the southern oil province of Khuzistan with its Arab ethnic majority, and Turcoman chiefs were said to be repossessing their land in the north-east which they had lost under the Shah's land reforms. Nasser Khan Qashqai, exiled in 1963 after the armed forces had broken the rising of the great Qashqai tribe against land reform, had returned to his tribal area.

Against this background I found Bakhtiar's resolute confidence and apparent belief that the people were responding to his government's programme admirable but grotesque: the Westernised opposition were as out of touch with the realities of the revolution as the Shah had been. My personal view was that it was all over, the revolution had won, and only one man might be able to bring about a peaceful transition to an Islamic Republic. This was Mehdi Bazargan, who had negotiated unsuccessfully with the striking oilworkers. He was old, about seventy-five, but he was one of the few secular leaders, educated in Europe, who had the confidence of the bazaar and the religious leaders including Khomeini. He had been a devoted adherent of Mossadegh and had been imprisoned by the Shah for his resolute leadership of the National Front in the early 1960s.

On January 21st my wife and I drove through the empty scarred streets, past walls bedecked with posters and graffiti, past shuttered shops and deserted government offices, past the plinths which had held the statues of the Shah and his father, to the airport to leave Tehran for good. The new Chief of Protocol of the Ministry of Foreign Affairs was present in the VIP lounge to see me off, a last courtesy. We said goodbye to the assembled staff and families of the Embassy with whom we had experienced so much, and departed.

A few days later I was at my desk in the Foreign Office, still concerned with Iranian affairs amongst many other responsibilities. But my impressionistic narrative ends here. My involvement with Iran persisted through my months in London and through the next three years when I was British Ambassador to the United Nations in New York and was faced with the American hostage crisis and the war between Iran and Iraq. But my deep personal engagement ended with the departure of the Shah and my own departure from Tehran and I was only a closely concerned spectator of the final days of the revolution. As all the world knows, Khomeini returned in triumph to Tehran on January 26th. For about two weeks there were two governments in the country, Bakhtiar's and Khomeini's provisional government under Mehdi Bazargan. On February 11th–13th the opposition pushed and the armed forces collapsed in a welter of bloodshed which took the life of one of my oldest and closest friends, Joe Alex Morris of the *Los Angeles Times*, victim of a stray bullet in the decisive clash at the Iranian air force base at Doshan Tappeh in the south-eastern suburbs of Tehran. This time it really was all over.

The time has now come for me to try to answer the questions which I briefly outlined in the introduction to this book: could we have been more perceptive in the years before the revolution and if so, should we have adopted different policies right up to the end and, finally, if we had, would it have made any difference either to British interests or indeed to the evolution of events in Iran?

SEVEN

Retrospect

We had the experience, but missed the meaning,
And approach to the meaning restores the experience
In a different form ...

T. S. Eliot, 'The Dry Salvages'

The Iranian revolution was an event which compared in magnitude to the French or Russian revolutions. It was no routine change of regime in a Third World country, the replacement of King X by General Y through the agency of a military coup d'état – the substitute for the ballot box in so many states – or the fall of an individual dictator leaving the nature of the state intact. The Iranian revolution encompassed the total collapse of an apparently powerful, centralised autocracy founded on and backed by united and loyal military force, and the emergence from its ruins of a completely different Iran in virtually all respects.

It is never possible to state that an historical process started on a specific date with a particular event but, for purposes of convenience, I choose the incident at Qom on January 9th 1978 as the point of departure for the upheaval which culminated on February 11th 1979 with the fall of the Bakhtiar government and the extinction of the last remnant of the Pahlavi regime. By this yardstick the Iranian revolution took place over a period of thirteen months from start to finish.

But it is idle to pretend that the seeds of the cataclysm were not germinating months if not years before the shots fired by the garrison in Qom led to the civilian deaths which in turn generated further riots, more deaths and eventually a cycle of destruction and civil disobedience which swept away the

131

mighty Shah together with the foundations which he and his father had constructed over more than sixty years. Why was it that the regime itself and the many outside observers such as foreign diplomats, Western academics, the press, and even the opponents themselves of the Shah's regime, failed to perceive – in the years before the incident at Qom, indeed up to the late summer or early autumn of 1978 – the monstrous plant which the soil of Iran was shortly to release? Why did I, with all my experience of the region, fail to see what was about to happen under my eyes?

So far as the regime is concerned, I think that the answer to this question is fairly simple. By the 1970s the Shah had become overweeningly self-confident and his attitude was reflected far down the hierarchy of the Iranian establishment. Since the early 1960s Iran had been remarkably free of the popular disturbances which characterised most countries, both developing and developed, during that period. There had been trouble on the university campuses and sporadic terrorism, but the people as a whole had appeared docile and at least acquiescent in the Shah's policies. He had manipulated the internal politics of Iran at will, experimenting with different systems without stimulating overtly hostile re-actions. He had destroyed the power of the tribal leaders and of the landowners and had got away with it. He had dispersed the Communist Party and the National Front and had got away with it. He had moulded the armed forces to his own strong and loyal model and had got away with it. He had created a new class of entrepreneurs, a new middle class and a new class of industrial workers; he had emancipated the rural peasantry; he was in the process of bringing prosperity and progress to the country as a whole. What could he have to fear from disgruntled students, surly mullahs and envious bazaar merchants? If he chose to liberalise at the end of 1976, what did it matter that the economy was faltering and that the expectations of the people had been disappointed? If there was trouble he could deal with it and if things got too turbulent for comfort, he could clamp down again with no difficulty. SAVAK was ubiquitous and well informed; he had his own private intelligence sources; the police and gendarmerie were his second line of defence and, if it got that far, the imperial Iranian armed forces would deal with any serious trouble.

This analysis is over-simplified but I believe that it represents the core of the Shah's thinking as well as that of the political leaders and the senior officers of the security and armed forces, probably also of the leaders of the various opposition groupings until fairly late in the day. Perhaps the most vivid illustration of the complacency of the regime vis-à-vis the Iranian people emerged in 1978 when we realised that the armed forces and police had no training in crowd control or internal security duties, no equipment to deal with civil unrest without resorting to the use of lethal weapons, no riot squads, no contingency plans, nothing. What was happening throughout the greater part of the world could not happen in Iran.

However, my main purpose in this chapter is not to analyse in detail the background to the blindness of the regime but to clarify the reasons for my own lack of perception. A conventional wisdom has grown up since 1979 that the Western Embassies were taken by surprise because of inadequate information. We had, so the argument runs, concentrated too exclusively on commercial work during the boom years and had neglected sufficiently to scrutinise the Iranian political scene. By the same token we had been so anxious not to offend the Shah that we had eschewed contact with the opposition and had thus fallen victim to the very complacency that blinded the regime. It was with this judgment in mind that I deliberately set out in the earlier chapters of this book to record my view of the internal political situation in Iran as I saw it at the time in each of the years before the revolution, without resorting to self-justificatory hindsight. I have faithfully adhered to this constraint and I have also, over the past four years, spent many hours in exacting self-interrogation.

I have come to the conclusion that our inability to anticipate what happened between January 1978 and February 1979 did not, in fact, result from lack of information. It is true, as I have pointed out, that the main priority of the Embassy in the period of my Ambassadorship was export promotion. It is equally true, as I have made clear, that we undertook our scrutiny of the internal scene with considerable discretion in order to avoid precipitating a crisis in our relations with the Shah. Nevertheless, as I have reconstructed my reporting in the years 1974–7, I have been surprised at the volume of material on the domestic situation, the number of times we addressed various contingencies and the detailed extent of our knowledge. Obviously if I had had more officers engaged on political work the quantity of factual material available to us would have been greater. However, I doubt whether this would have done more than confirm what we knew already. As I hope that I have already indicated, we did identify the principal elements of opposition to the Shah, namely the religious classes, the bazaar and the younger generation of the intelligentsia. We were aware that the old political parties – the communists, the National Front, etc. – would never forgive him for what he had done to them in the 1950s. We were under no illusions about the popularity of the regime, and recognised that by 1976 the pangs which were inevitably accompanying the transformation of Iranian society, combined with the disappointment of expectations attendant on the collapse of the oil boom, had created a serious and widespread malaise. Where we went wrong was that we did not anticipate that the various rivulets of opposition, each of which had a different reason for resenting the Shah's rule, would combine into a mighty stream of protest which would eventually sweep the Shah away. And, even if we had foreseen this combination, we would probably have concluded that purely civilian opposition, however united and however vocal, would be powerless against the bulwark of the armed forces, provided that they remained united and loyal to the Pahlavis.

Hence I am inclined to think that our lack of perception derived not from a failure of information but from a failure to interpret correctly the information available to us. We were looking down the right telescope but were focused on the wrong target. Here I blame myself unreservedly. Although I had the academic background to lead me to a correct interpretation of the facts which we had identified, I did not draw the appropriate lesson from Iran's historical past but generalised overmuch from my experience in Turkey and the Arab world. Let me explain. From the Middle Ages until the twentieth century, the regular armed forces were at the centre of power in the Ottoman Empire. First this meant the dreaded Janissaries, the scourges not only of the Empire's foes but of the Ottoman Sultans themselves. Next, after the overthrow of the Janissaries in the early nineteenth century, the modernised regular army ruled the Ottoman roost, as exemplified by the Young Turks revolution in the early 1900s and Kemal Atatürk's seizure of power in the 1920s. To this day the Turkish armed forces, as we have seen more than once since they overthrew the government of Adnan Menderes in 1960, have constituted the determining factor in the politics of the Turkish Republic. The Arab states which emerged in the 1920s, as the successors to the Ottoman Empire in the Middle East, inherited this tradition. We have become familiar with military coups d'état in Syria, Iraq, Egypt, Libya, etc. – even King Hussein's power in Jordan rests to a great extent on the loyalty of the Jordan Arab army. Hence it has become a truism that the permanence or otherwise of most Arab governments depends on the loyalty of the armed forces, and the attention of outside observers is directed principally to assessing whether or not this loyalty is likely to break down, thus leading either to civil war or more likely to the substitution of one military or quasi-military leader for another.

However, the Iranian tradition has been different ever since Iran re-emerged as a nation state at the beginning of the sixteenth century. Until the nineteenth century successive Shahs depended for their military strength on feudal and tribal levies: their survival or otherwise, like that of English kings before the Civil War, derived from their ability to command the loyalty of 'barons' rather than the loyalty of regular forces directly answerable to the Crown. In the nineteenth century the Qajar Shahs developed the beginnings of a modern army but their hold on power was still based on their political skill in balancing and controlling civilian groups which were disposed to compete with the throne for power. The religious leadership, together with tribal chieftains and rural landowners, had been the most influential of these elements ever since Shi'ite Islam became the state religion of Iran in the sixteenth century with the advent of the

Safavid dynasty. In the nineteenth century, with the first seeds of modernisation beginning to break surface, the small nucleus of Westernised intellectuals emerged as another challenge to the absolutism of the Shah. In addition the bazaar merchants who controlled the levers of the traditional economy of the country constituted a third force. The bazaaris were historically the allies of the mullahs through a symbiosis which persisted through until 1978. The mullahs relied, and still rely, largely on the bazaar for the financial contributions which enabled them for centuries to operate what amounted to a state within the constituted Iranian state. The bazaaris depended and still depend on the mullahs since they know that, if they fall foul of them, the mullahs can rouse the devout and fanatical urban artisan and working classes against them.

On a number of occasions during the nineteenth and early twentieth centuries these three elements – religious, intellectual, bazaari – combined to oppose some action of the Shah or to promote some cause on which they were, albeit temporarily, united. Three examples come to mind. In 1872 Nasruddin Shah granted a far-reaching concession to a naturalised British businessman, Baron de Reuter, which would have given him a monopoly covering almost all aspects of the Iranian economy. Under pressure from the clergy and the liberal politicians, the Shah was obliged to cancel the concession. In 1891–2 Nasruddin Shah granted a monopolistic tobacco concession to a British company. The clergy and the bazaar merchants combined to oppose this move, and the liberals disseminated pamphlets throughout the country attacking the concession. Scattered protests followed which developed into countrywide rioting. Finally the clergy decided upon a campaign of civil disobedience and called on the Faithful to abandon smoking until the concession was cancelled. The ban was widely maintained to the extent that even the Imperial Household gave up smoking. In the end the Shah was forced to back down and the concession was withdrawn. In the Constitutional Movement of 1905–6 the intelligentsia, the merchants and the clergy again combined to overcome the Shah's resistance to the granting of a constitution. Their methods included civil disobedience and the withdrawal of co-operation from the central government. This took the form of mass movements into various 'sanctuaries' including the grounds of the British Legation where more than 10,000 Tehran notables camped for some weeks. With the country paralysed, the Shah was forced to climb down and to grant the 1906 constitution which was still, at least in theory, the basis of government until the Shah was ousted in 1979.

It is fascinating to compare these distant events with what happened between January 1978 and February 1979. The similarities are striking. In the late 1970s, as on the previous occasions, the same groups – clergy, intellectuals and bazaaris – were alienated from the regime for their own differing reasons. Shortly after the Shah, through his policy of liberalisation, allowed this suppressed opposition to make itself heard, these disparate elements united with the objective of bringing the Shah to his knees. Even the tactics employed were the same. Scattered protests developed into country-wide rioting followed by civil disobedience – the strikes which progressively paralysed the country from September/October 1978 until after the Shah's departure in January 1979. It was, I have always believed, the strikes more than anything else which brought about the collapse of the regime. The armed forces remained broadly loyal to their Commander-in-Chief to the bitter end, but they were helpless to combat nationwide civil disobedience. The clergy, as in 1872, 1892 and 1906, provided the organisation and, aided by modern communications, were able to conduct their campaign with even greater effectiveness than they had displayed against the Shah's Qajar predecessors.

Why did I not apply these lessons of history, which were part of my intellectual knowledge of Iran, to the contemporary scene? Should I not have calculated, as early as 1974, that, if opposition to the Shah grew beyond a certain point, it would manifest itself according to the well established Iranian tradition, that is to say that disparate and seemingly mutually incompatible opposition groups would not remain fragmented and ineffective, but would combine and furthermore would employ tactics which would neutralise the Shah's power base – the armed forces and the security services? It does not surprise me that the Shah and his supporters did not make this calculation. In so far as the Shah had a sense of his country's history, he spurned comparison with the events of the nineteenth century. In his eyes Qajar Iran was contemptible, weak and redolent of the worst characteristics of a foreign-dominated Islamic state in a condition of virtual dissolution. He and his father had changed all that and his historical memory had vaulted back over 2,000 years to the days of Cyrus the Great when the state was protected, internally and externally, by the 'Immortals', the regular army of the time, of which his imperial armed forces and particularly the Imperial Guard were the modern manifestation. It is significant in this context that, even at our farewell meeting on January 8th 1979, he vigorously repudiated my analogy of the revolution with the fate suffered by the Qajar Shahs at the hands of the same combination of forces which had brought him down.

But I, who had never swallowed the Shah's version of Iranian history, should have known better. I have brooded long on this error of interpretation and have come to the following conclusions. First, as I have already suggested, I had become too accustomed to observing the principle of the primacy of military force in the politics of the countries in which I had served to be able to make the intellectual leap necessary to take into account the uniqueness of Iran in this regard. In a nutshell I made the mistake of particularising about Iran from the general trend of my previous experience. It was not that I failed to scrutinise the possibilities of the collapse of the regime. I frequently analysed what might happen if the Shah disappeared from the scene through natural causes, illness, accident or assassination. I kept a close eye on the loyalty of the armed forces but always concluded, rightly as it turned out, that the ingredients which had so often led to military intervention in other countries were lacking in Iran and that the Shah could reasonably count on their continued loyalty, even to his successor if he should suddenly be removed by whatever cause.

Secondly, I overestimated the extent to which sixty years of Pahlavi rule had transformed the nature of Iranian social and political life. The Shah's father, Reza Shah, had broken the pattern by coming to power through military action. The circumstances were exceptional in that Iran in the first two decades of the twentieth century had virtually lost its status as an independent geo-political entity. Central government was almost non-existent and Reza Shah had no difficulty in seizing power since he commanded the only disciplined force in existence in northern Iran at the time – the Persian Cossacks who had been abandoned by their Czarist Russian officers after the Bolshevik Revolution. Reza Shah had built a modern army as his power base first to unify and thereafter to rule the country and his son had built strongly on this foundation. Mohammed Reza Shah had also undertaken a major programme of modernisation which appeared on the surface to be having some effect throughout the labyrinth of Iranian society. I was inclined to think therefore, while dismissing the ballyhoo about Pahlavi Iran being a renaissance of the pre-Islamic Persian Empire, that there had been a genuine severance with the immediate pre-Pahlavi past and that contemporary Iran had evolved on the pattern of superficially similar, military based, Third World autocracies in a condition of rapid economic and social development. This mistaken judgment led me to the conclusion that, provided the Shah could continue to depend on his powerful and loyal armed forces, he was safe from the assaults of fragmented and unarmed civilian elements however implacably hostile they might be. I continued to hold this view until late September 1978 and it was only when the political strikes began that I realised that history was indeed beginning to repeat itself. By that time it was too late for this revelation to be of much practical use.

Had I been more perceptive in the years before the revolution, that is to say had I appreciated that the forces of opposition could be more formidable than I thought and the Shah's power base less solid in combating them, should I have recommended that the British government adopt different policies towards Iran? I think not. We were never in doubt that, as with most Third World regimes, the Shah could disappear overnight to be replaced by a government less responsive to British and Western interests. We thought this unlikely but we never discounted the possibility. We also realised that, by the very nature of the regime, we could not expect to reap the maximum rewards from our relationship with Iran unless our relationship with the Shah was close and unclouded by suspicion of our commitment to him. This involved a risk but I still believe that we were right to take it. The plain fact is that Pahlavi Iran was, in the short term, a valuable ally for Britain as well as being a highly lucrative market. The relative tranquillity and pro-Western orientation of Iran from the mid-1950s until the late 1970s was of cardinal importance at a time when the rest of the region – the Arab Middle East and the Indian sub-continent – was in a state of intermittent turmoil, vulnerable to Soviet penetration and hence potentially dangerous to crucial British material interests. For example, co-operation with Iran was essential to the maintenance of the status quo in the independent states of the Persian Gulf in the years immediately following our withdrawal at the end of 1971. Setting aside the question of price, it was of the utmost importance to Britain that we could rely on the flow of Iranian crude oil at a time when Arab oil was susceptible to political boycotts. Furthermore, between 1974 and 1978 Iran was Britain's largest export market in the Middle East, contributing thousands of millions of pounds sterling in foreign exchange at a time of great need. I could continue to cite many such examples both in the political and commercial fields and there is no doubt in my mind that, had we adopted a more equivocal attitude towards the Shah in the light of a more pessimistic assessment of his chances of survival, many of these benefits would not have accrued to us. To sum up, we gambled on the Shah and, for many years, our gamble paid off. I have no regrets on this score.

This leads me to a further question. Notwithstanding the imperfection of our analysis of the internal situation, should we have forced our advice on the Shah before he divested himself in the late summer of 1978 of his reluctance to discuss Iranian domestic politics with outsiders, particularly ourselves? I find this a difficult question to answer. On the one hand it can be argued that the British stake in Iran had become so important by the mid-1970s that a collapse of the regime would be of direct concern to British national interests. Therefore, if we believed that the situation was deteriorating and that the regime was making mistakes, surely it was our duty to our own country to speak out regardless of the Shah's inhibitions and obsessive suspicion of 'the British'. On the other hand, I regarded it as an important point of principle that we could only hope to establish a normal relationship with Iran, such as we enjoy with, for example, our Western European partners, if we buried the past and demonstrated to the Shah that we did not consider that we had any more right either to interfere in or to advise on internal political questions than, say, the French Ambassador in London had to involve himself in British domestic politics. Additionally, there was the problem of the Shah's character, another area in which our analysis proved less than accurate. By the 1970s we and other foreign governments had come to accept as genuine the character which the Shah had constructed for himself. In spite of our knowledge of his vacillations and weaknesses as a young man, of his demonstrable lack of charisma as a popular leader, we regarded him as he wished to be regarded, as a masterful, formidable autocrat, knowledgeable, skilful, in control of events and fiercely sensitive about his and his country's independence of foreign tutelage. We accepted him in this image and believed, rightly, that he would resent and strongly react to any attempt to advise him on how to conduct Iran's affairs. We believed that any gratuitous attempt to advise him, especially coming from us, would cloud our relationship and damage our national interests. I am convinced that this was a true assessment and that, if we had tried to suggest to the Shah at any time before 1978 that he adopt or avoid certain courses of action, we would have received a bloody nose and our competitors would have reaped the benefit of our discomfiture. At that period, there was ferocious competition between the individual countries of Western Europe, North America and Japan for the Iranian market and we could not risk anything which might have put us at a disadvantage at a time when the Shah personally controlled the distribution of major development contracts. The risk might have been worth taking if we had had any confidence that our advice would have been heeded. But we had no such confidence. On the contrary there is little doubt that we would have succeeded only in exciting resentment and suspicion. I sometimes used to think that, in a more sensible world, the representatives in Tehran of the Western industrial nations and Japan should get together, come to a common assessment of the internal dangers to the regime, secure unified instructions from their respective governments and make a collective *démarche* to the Shah. This would have had two advantages. Such a *démarche* might by its nature have influenced the Shah, and he would not have been able to penalise any individual country. But I regarded such a diplomatic exercise as utopian. In the competitive and gossipy atmosphere of Tehran in the boom time, it would have been difficult enough to have arranged the initial meeting of about fifteen Ambassadors (who would have taken the initiative?), still more so to reach meaningful consensus on what we should say, and even harder to secure the approval of fifteen governments and so on. I recall that, in the monthly meetings of the Ambassadors of the European Community, internal affairs were seldom discussed. Each of us feared that critical comment would be seized upon and exploited to the commercial disadvantage of whoever had been incautious enough to speak his mind!

Another factor, also related to our misinterpretation of the Shah's character, was our assumption that he must be better informed about the domestic situation in his own country than we were. We had experienced his shrewdness and mastery of foreign and strategic matters and not unnaturally concluded that, with all the information-gathering facilities at his disposal, he was also master of internal affairs. On the few occasions, one or two of which I have described in earlier chapters, when I ventured to touch on a specific area of obvious discontent, I took his haughty rejection of my remarks as a thinly disguised way of telling me to mind my own business. It never occurred to me, until the intimacy of 1978 revealed the staggering remoteness of his thinking from the realities which surrounded him, that he actually believed the unconvincing theories which he advanced to me, a conspicuous example being his statement that the widespread student discontent was only a minority manifestation stimulated by a handful of foreign-inspired agitators.

Four years later and with the benefit of hindsight, I con-

clude, as I did at the time, that it would have been impossible
for us, or indeed for any other friendly power, to have inter-
vened successfully with the Shah before 1978. He had become the slave of the personality which he had created for
himself and had built a wall between himself and his foreign
friends, as he had against his own most loyal Iranian advisers,
to protect himself against criticism which, as he grew in
power and prestige, became increasingly intolerable to him.
But this leads me directly to the final question. When the tide
of revolution was flowing and his wall of arrogance and imperial remoteness collapsed, is there anything which we, individually or as part of a collective Western effort, could have
done by way of advice or action which might have checked
the flood and enabled him to survive even though with the
reduced powers afforded to the Iranian monarch under the
constitution of 1906? By the late summer of 1978 his barriers
had come down and he was anxiously seeking our advice and,
a fortiori, that of my American colleague. Equally we realised
that his original character had not changed, that he was still
indecisive and lacking in the bloody resolution which char-
acterises the traditional autocrat, and that he had a pathetic
and altogether mistaken belief that the Americans and the
British, if not determined for their own arcane and incom-
prehensible reasons to overthrow him, must somehow have
the ability to maintain him on his throne.

Since the revolution there has been a considerable amount
of rhetoric, particularly in the United States, about how
America 'lost' Iran, about how the West, particularly the
Americans, 'allowed the Shah to be toppled' or even encouraged his downfall. These sentiments are not only current
amongst Iranian exiles where, as I suggested in the preface to
this book, the view is widely held that the Iranian people by
themselves were incapable of overthrowing the mighty Pahlavis and that the revolution must have come about through
a deep-laid American or British plot. A preferred, and to us
flattering analysis is that the Americans, who had the greater
physical power, were the actual instruments, acting under
the direction of the wily British. Our motives, as I understand
them from my Iranian friends, were related either to oil or to
the need to check the spread of communism or both. We had

never forgiven the Shah for breaking the British monopoly of Iranian oil in the 1950s; we had never forgiven him for master-minding the price increase in December 1973; we needed by 1978 to reduce the overall supply of OPEC crude oil in order to bring about a shortage and thus increase the profits of our own oil companies; we believed that a theocracy would be a more effective bulwark against atheist communism following the communist takeover of Afghanistan than progressive, modernising Pahlavi Iran. Quite apart from this grotesque balderdash, the not unnatural product of two centuries of European meddling in Iranian affairs combined with the contempt of the Pahlavi establishment for the Iranian people, plus a psychological refusal to admit that the downfall of the regime was a consequence of its own mistakes, a surprising number of intelligent and well informed Europeans and Americans still adhere to the view that the United States and to a lesser extent Britain 'lost' Iran or that we could have 'saved the Shah'. It would be facile to dismiss this theory out of hand.

I believe it to be the case that, if the Shah had not 'liberalised' at the end of 1976, he would still be on his throne, or rather his son would if the Shah had in the meantime died of cancer. It was the gradual and increasingly uncontrollable release of opposition which followed the liberalisation that enabled the disparate forces to create the momentum which, when they combined, eventually proved irresistible. If the lid of repression had been kept as tightly screwed down as the Shah had kept it for many years previously, the opposition would have been unlikely to be able to make the all-important first steps. If, therefore, as I have never fully accepted, the Shah liberalised under pressure from the United States government, it can be argued that this was an error of judgment. If, which I do not know, there was prior consultation between Washington and Tehran about liberalisation as Western public pressure mounted against the tyranny and human rights abuses of the Pahlavis, it might have been more expedient to advise the Shah to postpone liberalisation until he could generate an upturn in the economy. By the end of 1976, as I have explained, there was a heavy malaise throughout Iran owing to the failure of the boom and the acute social and economic problems which it had stirred up in its wake. It was, in terms of the Shah's survival, the worst moment at which to raise the political lid. However, I would, as a Western European, have found it impossible to recommend to London, and my government would have found it equally impossible to concur in such advice, that we should oppose a decision by the Shah to allow more freedom of expression and to ease up on repression of his people. The same would no doubt have been true of President Carter who was elected on November 4th 1976 and inaugurated as President of the U.S.A. in January 1977. Equally I do not believe that, at that stage, the Shah would have been susceptible to direct advice either from the Americans or from ourselves. I am inclined to think that there was nothing which either of us could have done, even if we had wished to do something, and that the likelihood was that the Shah had decided to liberalise for his own reasons, a secondary consideration in his mind being that to do so would help to ingratiate him with the new American administration which was from the outset trumpeting its belief in human rights, democracy and the evils of over-arming Third World dictatorships, however friendly.

This brings me to the final phase of the revolution, the period between September 1978 and January 1979 when my American colleague and myself were seeing the Shah many times each week, sometimes together, sometimes individually, for uninhibited discussion of the mounting crisis. Knowing all that we now know, should I have offered the Shah different advice to that which I gave him and, if so, what should I have said? I dismiss the possibility that either we or the Americans or both could conceivably have saved the situation by any kind of intervention. By 1978 Third World countries like Iran had become stronger and less dependent on outside powers, and the influence of the Great Powers had waned relative to that which they had possessed in previous generations. The purchase of the loyalty of bazaar mobs, romantic secret operations, the minatory movements of fleets or armies, could be, and indeed were from time to time, effective in the early 1950s. I am convinced beyond a shadow of doubt that such exercises would have been not only futile but counter-productive in the radically different circumstances of 1978. In this context I remember, I think it was in November 1978, how the news of the movement of one American aircraft carrier from the Philippines to Singapore immediately stimulated an acceleration in the pace of opposition to the Shah, so far was it removed from overawing the populace. Those who think otherwise, and there are many, both Iranian, British and American, are in my judgment inhabiting a world of long-dead romantic illusions. The fact is that what happened in 1978 was a contest between Iranians and Iranians and that the intervention of outsiders could only have made things worse. The age of the distribution of dollar bills in oriental bazaars had gone.

But this consideration does not apply to the private advice which I and my American colleague were giving the Shah. It is not for me to explore the American position although I have touched on the divisions which emerged within the administration. Ambassador Sullivan, my good friend and colleague, has already developed this theme in his book, *Mission to Iran*. I will confine myself to my own, lesser, part in the drama and I have already described in detail some of the many discussions which I had with the Shah over those decisive four months. In his book, *Answer to History*, the Shah has implied that he did not believe in the sincerity of my advice and that he could not clear his mind of his obsessive suspicion that I was the front-line instrument of some devious British plot to rob him of his throne. But I can only repeat that the advice I gave him was genuinely personal and based on my best judgment of events in a country in which I had served continuously for nearly five years. Indeed, I can still hear my own voice telling the Shah on numerous occasions that I would not tell him what I thought unless he assured me that he would accept what I had to say as the disinterested advice of a genuine well-wisher, untainted by any ulterior motive. He invariably gave me such assurances, although I now know, as I suspected at the time, that he was intellectually and emotionally incapable – who can blame him in the light of his own history? – of accepting my views at their face value. So far as my government was concerned, they accepted that, as the man on the spot, I was best qualified to judge what advice to offer in a rapidly changing situation.

I cannot recall a time when I was told by London that I should have said something different or when I received specific instructions to take a certain line. I can only assume that, as I was faithfully reporting what passed between me and the Shah, my masters in London agreed with the general thrust of my arguments; I would certainly have been told so if they did not.

Strangely enough in the light of much that has been written after the event, the Shah and I were never in disagreement about the line of policy which should be followed if there was to be any hope of weathering the storm. From the moment when the nationwide strikes began for economic reasons in late September, I became convinced that there was no military solution to the crisis. The Shah was of the same mind. I can hear him saying, time and again, 'A military solution is no solution,' and 'A dictator can survive by killing his people: a king cannot.' Quite apart from moral considerations, I was certain that the notion of a military crack-down was an irrelevancy. The army could, and to a greater or lesser extent did, clear the streets and keep public disorder within more or less manageable limits, except for their deliberate failure to prevent the burning of Tehran on November 5th and during the final weeks when their morale, together with the whole state apparatus, was crumbling away. But what produced this eventual erosion of authority and the sapping of military morale, in brief what brought about the collapse of the regime, was not civil disorder but civil disobedience and passive resistance. No amount of military force, short of the progressive execution of hostages such as might well have happened in Nazi Germany or Soviet Russia, could force people to work. Thank God there was never any question of that kind of cold-blooded butchery in Iran under the Shah. When the strikes became political, the country died and only political measures could bring it back to life. I knew this from late September onwards and so did the Shah. Even General Azhari and his military colleagues, who resented the search for a political solution while Sharif-Emami was Prime Minister and who were disposed to believe that a few more whiffs of grapeshot would solve everything, were quickly disillusioned when they, by their own action, found themselves holding the reins of government. After his first week or two in office, Azhari searched for a political solution which would have enabled the military to return to their barracks as vigorously as had his predecessor, Sharif-Emami.

Hence the direction of my advice to the Shah, which coincided with his own judgment, was consistent from the major turning point of the Jaleh Square shootings on September 8th, to the end. Initially I believed that Sharif-Emami was right to try to outdistance the opposition and reclaim the initiative through making political concessions – the freeing of the press, lifting of censorship, release of political prisoners, revitalising and publicising parliamentary proceedings, abrogation of unpopular legislation and so on. This may have amounted to 'feeding the crocodiles' as Sullivan puts it, but there was hope that the crocodiles might be sated before they had eaten everything. And, as I saw it, the moment for effective military repression – the replacement of the lid – had passed with the discovery (or the rediscovery in Iranian historical terms) of the efficacy of passive resistance. When Sharif-Emami had plainly shot his bolt by late October, I thought that the Shah was right to try to construct a transitional coalition government to include moderate opposition elements such as the National Front, with the object of holding early elections leading to the full restoration of the 1906 constitution. When this initiative failed through the defection of the National Front leaders to the Khomeini camp and when the generals made their move on November 5th, I conceded that the Shah had no choice but to appoint a military Prime Minister despite his and my misgivings. I had already encouraged him to try to form a transitional government of neutral elder statesmen untainted either by party affiliations or by association with the regime over the previous twenty-five years, if the coalition initiative failed. I considered him right to revert to this proposition within days of General Azhari's appointment. The Shah and I had frequently agreed that, if this last chance failed, there were no further options in sight. He continued to try to form a government under Sadeghi until Christmas, and nearly succeeded. His hopes had been declining steadily from November onwards and I believe that, once the Sadeghi plan failed, he knew that the end had come. I do not think that the Shah, any more than myself, had any faith in a Bakhtiar government and he knew well that, once he left the country, the game was up.

I have been accused of persuading him to leave when he should have stayed. The truth is that I was surprised at his willingness to leave. For some time we in the Embassy had been debating whether or not the Shah was Lord Jim. It will be remembered that Joseph Conrad's Lord Jim was a young officer of the merchant navy with romantic and highly coloured visions of the perfect personality – calm and courageous in the face of danger, authoritative and composed when others were losing their heads, a model of the Victorian virtues. He longed to be presented with an opportunity to demonstrate to himself and to the world that he was worthy of his visions. But, at his first opportunity when the ship of which he was Chief Mate struck a submerged wreck, he jumped into a lifeboat in a fleeting moment of panic along with the other disreputable officers, leaving the hundreds of passengers – pilgrims to Mecca – abandoned on the sinking ship. The S.S. *Patna* did not sink, but there was an enquiry and Jim lost his commission and, more important, his own estimation of himself as the ideal personality which he had created in his mind. He spent the rest of his life trying to redeem his one moment of weakness and only found ultimate triumph in voluntarily facing a certain death which he could without difficulty or loss of honour have avoided. 'Not in the wildest days of his boyish visions could he have seen the alluring shape of such an extraordinary success! For it may very well be that in the short moment of his last proud and unflinching glance, he had beheld the face of that opportunity – which, like an Eastern bride, had come veiled to his side.'

I thought that the Shah probably would be Lord Jim. He had jumped ship in 1953 and had spent the subsequent twenty-five years redeeming this act by turning himself into a respected and dynamic world leader and by creating for himself a character consonant with his highest visions. I anticipated that, if the second opportunity came, he would die in his palace rather than suffer the humiliation of jumping ship for the second time. I was wrong, but it was not for me to encourage the Shah to re-enact the part of a Conradian hero. As I have recorded in my account of our last conversation on January 8th, the Shah insisted that I select the least disastrous of three equally hopeless options. I did so sincerely and under protest and I still believe that what I said was right. In any case, by that time he had conditioned himself into acceptance of a second, and this time permanent exile.

I reproach myself for many things during my five years in Iran, as I hope I have been candid enough to admit in this book. But I do not reproach myself for the advice I gave the Shah during those last four months. Given the same circumstances and even with the benefit of hindsight, I would say the same again. Each attempt to halt the onrushing tide was overwhelmed but each attempt was justified and indeed might have succeeded up to the decisive day of November 5th. The odds were long but, until the generals made their terrible blunder, there was a chance that the Shah might survive as a constitutional monarch with greatly reduced powers, perhaps the best possible outcome for Iran. After November 5th, with the advent of the military government, my hopes declined almost to zero and I believe that the Shah felt the same. Even so he was right to continue the search for a political solution to the end in spite of his mounting certainty of defeat. Above all he was right to reject the advice of his rash and foolish loyalists to unleash the armed forces against the people. God knows, the civilian casualties in the year of the revolution were heavy enough. It is to the eternal credit of the Shah that, right up to January 16th, he refused to contemplate a greater bloodbath which both he and I knew would have availed him nothing. I can say with all honesty that, through all the years of our long acquaintance, I never liked nor admired him so much as I did during those last months as he faced with sangfroid, objectivity, humour and above all with humanity the successive waves of crisis which were eventually to batter down his defences. Many of those who deserted his cause in his hour of need and either fled or cast their lot with what they believed to be the winning, even the better, side must now be filled with boundless regret.

Epilogue

What might have been is an abstraction
Remaining a perpetual possibility
Only in a world of speculation.

T. S. Eliot, 'Burnt Norton'

Throughout this book I have used the word 'revolution' to describe the events in Iran between 1978 and 1979. Indeed, as I have suggested, the scale of the political earthquake which left behind it an entirely different landscape in Iran was equal to, if it did not surpass, that of the two great revolutions of modern European history, the French and the Russian. However, I now believe that there has been only one revolution in Iran since the sixteenth century, namely that carried out by Reza Shah Pahlavi and built upon by his son, Mohammed Reza Shah Pahlavi. I define a revolution as the destruction of an established society and its replacement by a fresh structure, demonstrably distinct from the old. Reza Shah achieved precisely this. He broke the previous pattern of Iranian socio-politics. He created a modern army on European lines, thus adding an important new element to the power structure of the country. He curbed the strength of the clergy and made a start towards replacing the age-old bazaar economy by a modern industrial and financial sector. He destroyed with his new armed forces the autonomy or semi-autonomy of the ethnic, tribal and feudal factions and established for the first time in the post-Islamic history of Iran a centralised state with the rudiments of Western-style administration and services. His son built rapidly and extensively on this foundation, particularly in the last fifteen years of his reign when he felt free of domestic competition from feudal landowners, tribal chieftains and the rest. By 1978, Iran was quickly developing from being an essentially agricultural state dotted with market towns into an urban society with relatively sophisticated financial and consumer services, an incipient industrial base, the beginnings of a welfare state with universal education and health services and so on – in short a very far cry from the medieval structure which Reza Shah had inherited sixty years previously.

What happened in 1978/1979 was therefore not a revolution but a counter-revolution, albeit sixty years after the original event. Ayatollah Khomeini has restored and gone beyond the socio-political structure which the Pahlavi Shahs deemed it essential to set aside if Iran was to have a progressive future along with the other nations of the region. Khomeini has re-established the twin pillars which dominated Iranian society for hundreds of years – the Shia Muslim religious hierarchy and the bazaar merchants. He has reached even further back than the nineteenth century when these two elements shared influence with the new class of Westernised intellectuals. Certainly the intelligentsia combined with Khomeini to overthrow the Shah. But, for the moment at least, a ruthless and savage policy of repression has eliminated the intelligentsia from the structure of power: they are either underground, quiet, dead, in prison or in exile. Mullahs and bazaaris reign supreme and Khomeini has even gone one step further than his predecessors, in that they always tolerated, to a greater or lesser extent, a secular ruler as representative of the temporal power. Now Khomeini has in effect become the Shah, the supreme and semi-divine leader. (This could prove an error. One of the Shah's problems was that, by destroying all the balancing elements in Iranian politics and by creating for himself a position of sole leadership in direct communion with the people, there was no one else for the people to blame when things went wrong.) The new constitution is a far more reactionary document than the constitution of 1906; the modern administrative and economic structure which the Pahlavis built has been shaken to its foundations and only the armed forces survive as evidence of the revolutionary achievements of the Shah and his father.

And the armed forces are, not necessarily through any fault of Khomeini, engaged in a war with their Iraqi neighbours of a nature which recalls the persistent struggle over four centuries between the Ottoman and Persian Empires in precisely the same area. To sum up, Khomeini appears to have achieved the difficult objective of running the time machine backwards for well over sixty years and establishing a counter-revolutionary regime which bears a remarkable resemblance to that of Iran in the eighteenth century. Something of the kind happened in France in the aftermath of the French Revolution and would no doubt have happened in Russia if the civil war had gone the other way. In the longer term I find it hard to believe that sixty years of revolutionary progress and transformation under the Pahlavis will be as though they never happened. So much of the change was welcome to large sections of the Iranian people – the emergence of a cash economy, the high wages in the new industries, the evolution of a consumer society, the emancipation of women, the eradication of personal insecurity in the rural areas, the freeing of the peasants, the new social services, mass education, and so on. If Khomeini fails to deliver all this and more, there may come a time when he or his successors will stand accused by the urban masses as the Shah did, and he may find that the regular army which he has inherited from the Pahlavis, notwithstanding the fanatical devotion of the Revolutionary Guards, will not, as it did for so long for the Shah, protect him against the wrath of the people. Perhaps he is wise to keep the bulk of the armed forces hundreds of miles from the capital, fighting against an external enemy.

Why did the Pahlavi revolution eventually fail and why was it, so many years later, still vulnerable to counter-attack from the identical forces which had combined against the Qajar Shahs so many years ago? It seems to me that the twin essence of success for revolutionaries is speed and ruthlessness. Traditional forces, with their deep roots in society, are tenacious and hard to eradicate. Lenin and Stalin knew this: hence the merciless massacre and displacement of dissident elements, for example the priests and Kulaks and national minorities such as the Chechens and the Ingush. Anyone who might threaten the Soviet regime was eliminated, regardless of numbers, and, at the close of a bloody civil war, the Soviet leaders had instruments in their hands which would not hesitate to carry out their will. Reza Shah was in an entirely different position. Personally he was a man of ferocious courage and awe-inspiring physical presence. He knew his enemies and did not hesitate to crush them as and when he could – many dissident politicians, seditious clergymen and tribal and ethnic leaders could testify to that. But he had to proceed slowly and with caution. Iran in the 1920s was too weak, too backward and lacking in resources (oil revenues from the British-owned oilfields in the south were trifling compared to the needs of a country the size of Western Europe) for Reza Shah to effect a violent and rapid transformation from the medieval economy of agriculture and the bazaar to a modern industrial base. Unlike his neighbour, Kemal Atatürk, he did not have the aura of a national hero which might have enabled him to use his power to destroy the state within a state which the Shia Muslim clergy had created over the centuries. Reza Shah made a start in these directions in the twenty years before he was forced to abdicate in 1941, but most of his energies had to be expended on reuniting the provinces under central government and in re-establishing fundamental law and order throughout the country. Atatürk, his revolutionary neighbour, who died a few years before Reza Shah's abdication, had cut deeper. He had two major advantages, first the prestige of a national hero and secondly the Turkish army, who were always ready to follow a nationalist leader. The Sunni Islamic clergy were a less formidable adversary than their Shi'ite counterparts and Turkey was more advanced socially and economically than Iran when Atatürk and Reza Shah seized power over their respective countries. Even so, the reaction came in Turkey in the 1950s and has persisted to this day. But the Turkish Republic is probably strong enough to survive without having to compromise Atatürk's revolutionary programme. In Reza Shah's case he had been unable to do much more than scratch the surface of Iran before he fell in 1941; by sheer force of personality he had tamed the traditionalist challengers but his adversaries were still intact and ready to threaten his successor. Mohammed Reza Shah acceded to the throne in the most unpromising circumstances with Iran occupied by Soviet and British troops. After the war he first had to devote himself to the reunification of the country by defeating the separatists who had been established in Kurdestan and Azerbaijan by the Soviet Union. He then faced a long struggle, lasting nearly twenty years, to establish personal ascendancy. It was not until the early 1960s that he felt able freely to resume his father's revolutionary progress. Yet even during his final fifteen years of unfettered power, and for all his desperate sense of urgency and the redoubling of the pace after the oil price rise of 1973, he fell far short of the goals which would have neutralised his implacable opponents, the clergy. It is true that he achieved a number of revolutionary aims, for example the destruction of the power of the landowners and tribal chiefs, the creation of a new entrepreneurial and technocratic class, and the establishment of an industrial base for the economy. But, since he had neither the strength nor the will physically to destroy the network of religious organisations, as the Russians would have done in similar circumstances, his objective of replacing the bazaar economy with a modern economic sector became all the more important. If he could have reduced the economic power of the bazaar to negligible proportions, the clergy would have been starved of funds and their quasi-statal organisation would either have withered or have been forced to draw its financial support from institutions such as the government itself or the Westernised entrepreneurs, which would then have called the tune instead of meekly contributing to the counter-revolutionary pressure of the extremist mullahs. However, first because of lack of resources and latterly because of lack of time and skilled manpower, the Shah never managed to reduce the traditional sector of the economy below about 70 per cent of the whole. In the last years, moreover, SAVAK reserved their harshest treatment for the students (thus alienating what could have been an important constituency for the Shah), the communists (a relatively insignificant threat), and dissidents in the modern industrial proletariat (perhaps the Shah's most ardent supporters). They seem to have largely ignored as unworthy of attention the powerful combination of bazaar and clergy which was ultimately to destroy the whole system.

The Shah fell between two stools. Even at the height of his authority he was not ruthless enough to destroy the clergy; nor could he transform Iranian society quickly enough to neutralise them. He was engaged in a relentless race and he calculated after 1973 that he had the means to outstrip the forces of Iranian reaction. But he failed. In the end they caught up with him and, when battle was joined, it transpired that the impact of the Pahlavi revolution had been so superficial that the urban masses preferred to turn to the leadership which represented their Islamic past and their Middle Eastern roots, rather than to support the man who was trying so hard to turn them into something which they were not. The Shah's constituency, their loyalty sapped by inflation and their staying power weakened by corruption and luxury, fell away until he was left only with his armed forces and a handful of devoted adherents. In the end the armed forces themselves collapsed, thus underlining the point that, even in the most tyrannical of dictatorships, there is a minimum level of popular acquiescence below which no regime can expect to survive.

Index

157